Excel

Get the Results You Want!

YEARS 7–10 ENGLISH

POCKET BOOK

AF872394

KRISTINE BROWN

Reprinted 2005, 2006, 2007, 2008 (twice), 2009, 2011, 2012

Updated in 2013 for the Australian Curriculum

Reprinted 2015, 2019, 2021

ISBN 978 1 74125 009 1

Pascal Press
PO Box 250
Glebe NSW 2037
(02) 8585 4044
www.pascalpress.com.au

Publisher: Vivienne Joannou
Project editors: Grant Bailey and Mark Dixon
Internal design and typesetting: Larissa Petryca, ID360
Additional typesetting by Grizzly Graphics (Leanne Richters)
Edited by Jessica Perini and Sue Harvey
Indexed by Puddingburn Publishing Services
Cover by DiZign Pty Ltd
Printed by Vivar Printing/Green Giant Press

Contents

Dear student,

This little book covers the important terms and concepts you need to understand if you want to do well in your English studies in Years 7–10.

The book is not intended to be read through from cover to cover. It is intended as a reference book to be looked at when you need help. An index has been included to help you find what you want.

It could be a good idea, however, to set aside time to read through **chapters 1 to 4**. These cover some important understandings about text, context and language. It won't take you long to read these chapters, and you can then refer back to them whenever you need to.

Chapters 5 to 11 will be most useful when you are studying particular kinds of texts such as poetry and drama. They give you general guidance on responding to these texts, and explain the key terms and concepts (arranged alphabetically). In some instances you are referred to a different chapter or section to find the meaning of a particular term.

Chapter 12 gives you general guidance on writing key texts such as essays, reviews, speeches, feature articles and short stories. In a small book of this kind, it is not possible to cover everything you will need to write well and creatively. You will need your teacher's guidance to do this. You may want to look at references listed in **Other resources** (see **page 184**) to get further help.

You should use **chapters 13 to 15** for help with the basic tools of grammar, punctuation and spelling as needed.

I hope you find the ***Excel*** *Years 7–10 English Pocket Book* useful. Good luck with your English studies.

Kristine Brown

CHAPTER 1

Understanding text

In your English studies, you will constantly hear about and be asked to talk about **texts**.

This chapter helps you understand exactly what a **text** is, and what it means to **compose** a text or **respond to** a text.

It also explains how texts can be grouped into **text types** and into the two broad categories of **factual texts** and **literary texts**.

What is a text?

A text is a connected 'chunk' of language that makes meaning in a particular situation.

A text might be spoken (a conversation, an announcement) or written (a letter, a notice on a wall). It might be very short (a road sign) or very long (a novel).

A text might use words only (an essay, a poem), or it might include visual images (a website, a newspaper cartoon) or sound (a film). A text might also include non-verbal methods of communication (body movements, facial expressions and hand gestures while speaking).

In the past, the word **text** was only used for written communication, but it is now used for communication of all kinds, including speech and film.

Note: The word **text** may also be used to refer to the words on a page (e.g. *I could see the pictures but I couldn't read the text—it was too faint*).

Look at these examples of texts.

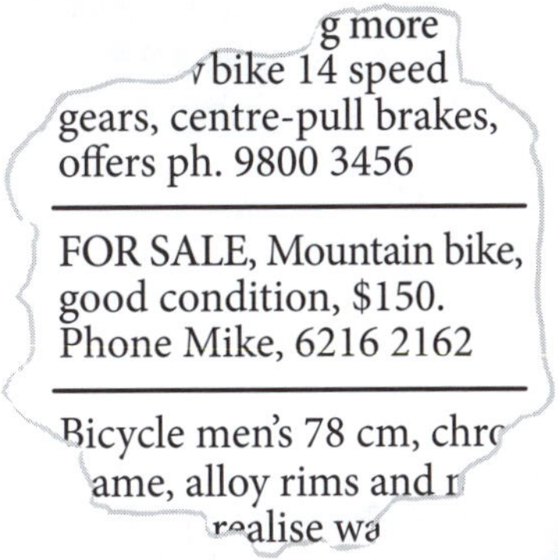
g more
bike 14 speed
gears, centre-pull brakes,
offers ph. 9800 3456

FOR SALE, Mountain bike,
good condition, $150.
Phone Mike, 6216 2162

Bicycle men's 78 cm, chr
ame, alloy rims and
realise wa

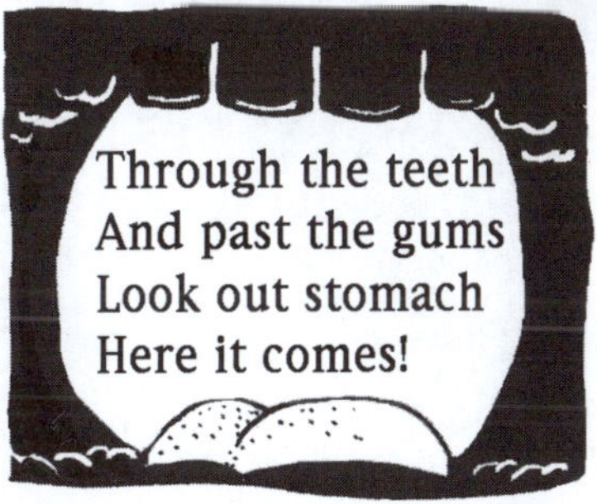

Attention passengers. The 7.20 service to the city has been cancelled due to a defective engine. The next train on Platform 2 will arrive at 7.50. We apologise for any inconvenience. Thank you.

NOT ASKING MUCH

Dear Editor,

Joe Rossi ("What about us oldies?") says that young people have too much money spent on them. Does he realise we are asking for a small concrete space for skateboarding —not an Olympic Sports Centre! The cost of a skateboard park is very, very small compared to other kinds of sports venues. Besides, it will probably be used by many more kids—giving them something healthy to do and keeping them out of muschief. You can't argue with that, Mr Rossi!

—Jay Idris, 15 years old

"Hey Jack"

"Hiya Laura.
See you at lunch?"

"OK."

Responding and composing

As a student of English you will spend a lot of time **responding** to texts and **composing** or **creating** texts of your own.

Responding to text

Responding to a text is the process of reading, listening to or viewing a text, and then talking or writing about it in some way. The term is a useful one for talking about *all* of these activities in a general way.

Responding involves talking or writing about:

- the meaning of the text (there may be many possible meanings)
- the language, structure and visual elements of the text
- the purpose of the text and its effect on its audience (including yourself)
- how the text relates to the world.

Sometimes when you respond to a text you might only have to talk or write about one of these things. At other times you might have to cover them all. It will depend on what your teacher asks you to do.

When we use the word **responding** we recognise that reading, listening to or viewing texts is in many cases a **subjective** process—that is, people will think about and react to a text in different ways. In your English studies, you will need to be able to explain your own personal reaction.

Composing text

Composing or **creating** a text is the process of producing a written, spoken, visual or other kind of text. Both terms are useful for referring to *all* of these activities. (They broadly mean the same thing, but your teacher may prefer one to the other.) In English, you will often be asked to create one text, such as a news report, in response to another text that you have studied in class.

Composing or creating a text involves:

- thinking about your purpose, your audience and other aspects of the context (see **chapter 2**)
- knowing how the type of text is usually structured
- knowing the kind of language that is usually used in this type of text
- planning, drafting and revising your text.

When we use these two terms we recognise that creating a text is a complex process. We also recognise that sometimes there is more than one person involved in the process. For example, an advertisement might involve an artist, a writer, a designer, a photographer and a director.

We can use the generic terms **composer**, **text creator** or sometimes **author** to talk about the person who creates a text. (Again, your teacher may have a preference about which term you use.) This person might be a writer, a poet, an advertiser, a film-maker, a cartoonist, a public speaker, a web-designer or, of course, yourself.

In your English class, you'll still hear about reading, writing, speaking and listening, and writers, speakers and poets, but you will often hear these other terms when your teachers (or textbook writers) are talking generally about all kinds of texts and want to include less traditional kinds of texts such as advertisements, cartoons or webpages.

In this pocket book, I'll generally use the terms **composers** or **text creators** when I want to talk in a general way about all kinds of people who produce texts. But I will use the more specific terms **writers**, **speakers**, **poets** or **film-makers** if I want to refer to the composers of a specific kind of text.

What is a text type?

Before you talk or write about a particular text, you need to be able to identify what type of text it actually is. That is, you need to be able to identify the **text type**.

Examples of text types are recipes, advertisements, warning signs, novels, myths, letters and emails, SMS text messages, webpages, bus timetables, poems, jokes, newspaper reports, notes, feature articles, interviews, radio talkback segments, debates, songs, fairy tales, information reports and play scripts.

Text types generally follow a particular structure and layout, and use language in a particular way. They also include particular kinds of information.

For example, a recipe is organised and written quite differently from a newspaper report. If a recipe were written like a newspaper report, the reader would find it difficult to follow, and no doubt make a few mistakes in the cooking process. Of course, the kind of information a recipe covers is different too. Not many newspaper reports are about what someone is cooking for dinner.

Composers don't structure a text and include particular kinds of information and language just for the sake of it. They do it because it serves their purpose in a particular communication situation.

When you are asked to **respond** to a text, it helps if you know what kind of structure and language is usually used in that type of text. This knowledge will also help when you are asked to **create** a particular type of text yourself. **Chapter 12** will help you to do this.

Sometimes composers play around with text types to create an original piece of writing. For example, a novel might be written as a diary. You might want to try this approach yourself in a creative writing task, but it is probably best to talk to your teacher about it first.

Look at this first draft of a classified advertisement. At the moment it reads like a personal conversation. Can you identify at least four things that need to be improved—in the content, structure and language—to make it more appropriate for the text type?

> I have a large fish tank that I wish to sell. It is not in great condition but you could easily fix it. At the moment I am using it for storing books so I am really looking for a quick sale. Ring me. 70709865

You probably thought about:

- putting the name of the sale item first
- using bold or capital letters to highlight some words
- leaving out unnecessary words
- adding details about the sale item (e.g. measurements, price)
- focusing on the good aspects of the sale item rather than the bad
- adding a name for readers to contact.

Informative, persuasive and imaginative texts

There are a number of ways to categorise texts. One way is to use three very broad categories: **informative** texts, **persuasive** texts and **imaginative** texts. Some texts are difficult to categorise this way because they cut across all three areas in purpose and content.

Informative texts

Informative texts (sometimes called **factual** texts) are texts that aim to provide us with useful information. They mostly contain facts but they might also include ideas and opinions. Generally their composers aim to inform, recount, instruct and describe.

Examples of factual texts are:

instructions
bus timetables
travel brochures
TV documentaries
historical documents
interviews
forms
surveys
meeting agendas
textbooks
newspaper reports
price lists
regulations
scientific reports
TV or radio news reports
SMS texts
information websites
job applications

Informative texts can be subdivided into **everyday texts**, **workplace texts** and **media texts**. Everyday and workplace texts are the kinds of texts you would see at school, home or work, or in the community. Media texts are texts that are intended to reach very large numbers of people via newspapers, radio, television or the internet, for example.

Which of the texts on pages 2–5 and page 11 would you call everyday texts and workplace texts? Which would you call media texts?

Imaginative texts

Imaginative texts (sometimes called **creative** or **literary** texts) are made up or invented by the composer with the main purpose of entertaining and interesting the audience. Examples are:

novels	short stories	TV dramas
ballads	cartoons	song lyrics
fables	limericks	play scripts
sonnets	folk tales	feature films

Imaginative texts express ideas in words, sound or visual images with the aim of interpreting our human experience and stimulating a response from us—an intellectual, emotional or imaginative response (or some combination of these).

Imaginative texts are generally fiction, but might sometimes contain, or be based on, fact. Some factual texts may be classified as imaginative also, because they use literary devices to achieve their aim (e.g. biographies). Other texts may similarly be difficult to categorise as clearly either factual or imaginative–Aboriginal dreamtime stories, for example.

Persuasive texts

Persuasive texts are texts which aim to put forward a point of view and persuade the audience that this view is valid, or texts which discuss issues that may help the audience reach a point of view. Examples are:

debates	feature articles
blogs	editorials
letters to the editor	political posters
advertisements	book reviews
discussions	essays

Persuasive texts use many different language techniques to express a point of view and to persuade the audience to think or behave in a certain way. They generally include some facts as well as reasoning to convince the audience.

CHAPTER 2

Understanding context

Every text is influenced by the fact that it is created at a particular time, in a particular place, and by a particular person with particular purposes, ideas, experiences and attitudes—in other words, every text is influenced by its **context**. This chapter helps you to understand this better.

What is context?

Context refers to the situation in which a text is composed. When you are talking about context, it is useful to think about these six areas:

- why the text was composed (**purpose**)
- who composed it (the **composer**, **author** or **creator**)
- who it was composed for (the intended **audience**)
- when and where it was composed and what was going on at the time (**social and cultural context**)
- what the text is about (the **subject**)
- how the text is communicated (the **mode**).

Whenever somebody creates a text, their choices about *what* to communicate and *how* to communicate are influenced by these six areas of context.

Think of your own communications. For example, you probably talk about different things, and talk about them in a different way, with your teacher than with your best friend.

When asked to respond to a text you should always think about the context in which it was composed, and how this might have influenced what was in the text and how it was expressed. You should also think about how **appropriate** the structure and language is to the context.

Look at the advertisement on page 16 and read the comments below about the choices the composer made based on the context. Do you think that the choices were appropriate? In other words, did they work?

- **Purpose** is to get a reader to take the dog home. The whole text is designed to achieve this purpose.
- **Composer** is the RSPCA, a respected animal welfare organisation. The headline mentions this to show readers that the information can be trusted. The local sponsor is also mentioned to reinforce this.
- **Audience** is the general community. Most readers will not be thinking about taking in a stray dog, but might be persuaded. The RSPCA therefore uses

RSPCA
waif of the week

"Hi, my name is Mozart. I'm a male Rotty 4 years old. I am great with other dogs big or small, I am everyone's friend. Even though I am a big dog, I am also great with kids. I love to play ball and will even give it back to you. I come desexed, vaccinated, wormed, heartworm tested and microchipped for $145 from RSPCA Blue Mountains Shelter, 121-125 Mort Street, Katoomba. 4782-2674."

Proudly sponsored by

FALLS HARDWARE, WENTWORTH FALLS

P617A

techniques to appeal to their emotions: use of the word *waif*; an appealing photo of the dog with eyes looking at the reader; use of the dog's 'own words' rather than a third person's description of the dog. Other information readers would want is also included, e.g. about vaccination.

- **Social and cultural context** is the fact that in our culture we keep dogs as pets, but do not always care well for them. Also, many people in the community are wary of rottweiler (rotty) dogs because of occasional attacks.
- **Topic** is a stray rottweiler dog. The dog breed affects the text—*waif* stresses the gentle side of the dog in contrast to reputation; *I am also great with kids* is included in the information; the photo shows a friendly looking dog.
- **Text mode** is mainly writing. The RSPCA has to attract readers and get across the dog's attractions in a very small space on a page filled with other advertisements. It uses a visual (photo) as well as language to achieve this.

Text purpose

Whenever you are asked to respond to a text, a useful way to begin is to ask yourself: *Why was this text created? What was the composer's purpose?*

We always have a purpose when we write, speak or otherwise communicate. Most of the time we communicate to:

- discuss ideas
- argue a point of view
- persuade someone to do something
- explain how or why something happened
- give factual information
- describe something
- give instructions
- recount what happened
- tell a story
- entertain.

Which of these was the main purpose of the RSPCA advertisement on page 16?

Sometimes we might have more than one purpose. For example, a novelist might want to tell a story, but at the same time raise awareness of an important social issue. Advertisers usually provide factual information about their products, but they are often less interested in informing readers than they are in persuading the readers to buy their products.

Do you think the RSPCA might have had another purpose in its advertisement? (Hint: Think about the problem of unwanted pets.)

The text purpose influences the language we use, but it also influences the way we **structure** or **organise** the ideas in texts.

For example, the RSPCA advertisement aimed to give information as well as persuade. But if informing had been its main purpose, it may not have given the information in one large block of text as in this advertisement. It may have, instead, broken it up into point form to make the information clearer to the readers.

Once you have thought about why the text was created, you can then ask yourself: *Did the composer achieve his or her purpose? How?*

For example, do you think the RSPCA would have achieved its purpose? That is, would a reader have taken in Mozart? Would *you* have taken him in?

1 To understand **how** composers achieve their purposes you need to look closely at language. **Chapter 3** will help you with this.

2 Sometimes you have to search quite hard to uncover a composer's real purpose. This is part of **critically responding** to the text. **Chapter 4** will help you with this.

The composer

In responding to a text, you should always ask yourself: *Who composed this text? How could the composer's identity have influenced the text?*

Note: your teacher may use the term 'author' or 'creator' for 'composer'.

If you asked ten people to write a page about animal welfare, for example, you would probably get ten very different responses. They might differ, for example, in:

- the facts selected for use
- the opinions expressed
- the emphasis given to particular information
- the tone (e.g. humorous, serious)
- the language used.

One of the most important reasons that texts differ is that the composers themselves differ. Different composers bring different points of view to the task of creating a text. The ten people writing about animal welfare would have had different experiences of life, and different kinds of knowledge about animal welfare. This would affect how they write about it.

Thinking about the composer is perhaps more important when responding to factual texts than to literary texts. You might ask: *Is the composer an expert? Is she or he an ordinary member of the community? Is she or he a member of a group or organisation with a particular view?*

Answers to these questions may well influence your response to the text. For example, as most advertisers are paid by the company advertising the product, it is not surprising that most advertisements describe the product in favourable terms. For this reason you may be less inclined to accept the accuracy of the factual statements about the product.

Of course, you cannot always know the exact identity of the composer. For example, in newspaper articles and on websites, the writer's identity is not always given. Uncertainty about the identity of the composer may cause you to question the reliability of the information.

When studying literary texts, knowing something about the composer can help you understand more fully the importance of the events and characters in the texts, such as why a poet or novelist wrote on particular subjects or themes. For example, knowing that Melina Marchetta, the author of *Looking for Alibrandi*, is from an Italian background helps you to appreciate the significance of the main character's experiences as a young girl of Italian background growing up in Australia, and her struggles with school, friends and a sense of identity.

Thinking about the composer is an important part of critically responding to texts. See **chapter 4**.

Audience

When responding to texts, you always need to ask: *Who is the audience? For whom was this text composed?*

Whenever we compose a text, we compose it **for** someone. We think about, for example:

- whether we know the audience personally
- what they *need* to hear or see
- what they *want* to hear or see
- what they expect in the structure and layout of the text
- what will make sense to them
- the way in which they think or feel about the topic
- the appropriate language for the audience.

Remember that *you* might not be a member of the **intended audience**—the people the composer imagined he or she was addressing. For example, it is important to keep in mind that novels written 200 years ago were written for readers living at that time rather than readers in the 21st century.

In responding to the text, you should distinguish between your response and the probable response of the intended audience. Ask yourself: *How might my response be different from the response of the intended audience*?

It is also important to consider the personal relationship between the composer and the audience, particularly when looking at texts composed by *one* person for *one* other person, such as a conversation or a letter. The feelings that exist between the two people and what has happened between them will influence the words used and the kinds of things talked about.

Once you have identified the audience, you should then consider how appropriate the text is for its audience. *In what ways was the text appropriate for this audience? In what ways was it inappropriate?*

For example, you might think the language of a speaker at a school assembly is too formal, or the language of a text for primary school children too complicated.

Look back at the RSPCA advertisement on page 16. *Who is the intended audience? Do you think the text was appropriate for this audience? In what ways?*

To understand **how** composers create texts to suit their audiences you need to look closely at language. You will get help with this in **chapter 3**.

Look at this extract. It is from the instruction booklet for a mobile phone.

Removing the SIM card

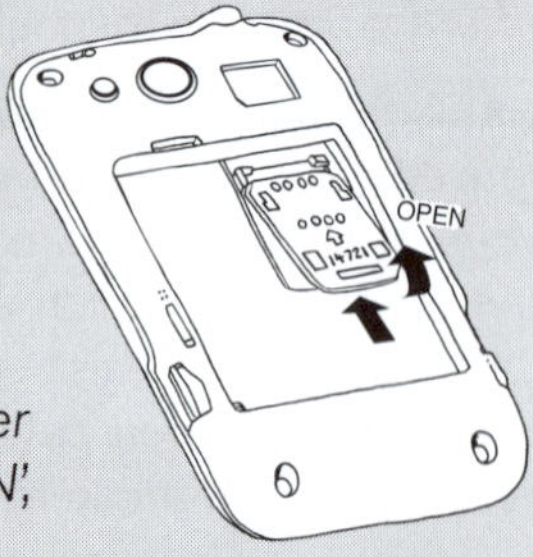

1. *Take the back cover off carefully. MAKE SURE YOU SWITCH OFF THE PHONE FIRST.*
2. *Remove the battery.*
3. *Slide the SIM card holder towards the word 'OPEN', then flip it open.*
4. *Slide the SIM card out from the SIM card slot.*

The writer of the manual understands their audience well. He or she:

- knows they are only interested in getting the phone set up, so the text focuses only on this
- knows that many people find mobile phone instructions difficult to follow, so has given the information in a way they will understand (e.g. simple words, headings, numbered steps)
- knows that the audience has no personal interest in the writer, so the text does not make personal comments or use personal language.

As a result, the text is very appropriate for its audience, its purpose and the overall context.

Social and cultural context

In responding to a text it is also important to ask yourself about the **social and cultural context** of the text: *When was the text composed? Where was the text composed? What was going on at the time?*

Social and cultural context largely refers to the 'big picture' and takes account of:

- the historical period
- the culture and way of life of the composer and their audience
- the attitudes and values of the society in which the text was composed
- important social issues, for example, civil war or revolution.

For example, Jane Austen's novels (e.g. *Pride and Prejudice*) were written in the early 19th century. The plots of all these novels revolve around the characters—female and male—seeking wealthy partners in marriage, or at least struggling with the dilemma of whether to marry for love or money. To understand the characters' motives and behaviour, it helps to know something about the inheritance laws at that time. These favoured the first-born male in a family against all other children, including females born before the first-born male. As a result, marrying into money was often the only way young women and men were able to survive financially.

Social and cultural context also includes the 'smaller picture'—that is, what was actually happening while the text was being created. For example, the content and language of a sports reporter's live broadcast of a match will be different from the content and language of an article about the same match written by the same reporter the next day. The difference will be partly to do with the fact that the match was actually happening at the time of the broadcast.

Look at this extract from an advice book for women in Australia in 1939:

> Home is the kingdom over which the wife should seek to reign as queen. So wholesome and attractive may the home be made by a contented, cheerful woman that the husband will leave it with reluctance, and will return to it at night, after the day's toil is ended, with naught but thoughts of quietness and peace. The possession of a sunny disposition is indeed a wife's most valuable asset, for it makes herself and all around her happy.
>
> Eulalia S Richards, *Ladies Handbook*

- *What can you say about the social and cultural context of this text? For example, what were the social attitudes to women's roles and men's roles at the time this advice was written?*
- *How have these influenced how the topic is written about?*

- *What differences can you see in the language of 1939 and that of today?*
- *How would a text on this topic be written today?*

Topic

The **topic** of the text might seem quite obvious, but it can in fact be quite complicated. You always need to ask yourself: *What is this text about?*

In literary texts, you will often have to look beyond the topic to think about the **theme**. For example, a story might be about a young boy who invents things, but the theme might be friendship in adolescence. You need to ask: *What does the composer really want me to think about?*

See **page 85** for more on literary theme.

In factual writing, it is sometimes very important to look beyond the obvious topic to see if there is a 'hidden' topic. This can be important to think about when reading newspaper articles, for example.

Identifying the topic is an important part of critically responding to texts. See **chapter 4**.

Mode

How the text physically reaches the audience is called the **mode** (or **medium**) of communication. (The word **media** is the plural of medium.) Examples of text modes are:

- spoken—face to face
- spoken—telephone
- written—on paper
- written—electronic (e.g. on computer, on mobile phone)
- interactive (texts you can change or manipulate, for example a computer game)
- visual (texts that include images)
- film
- mass media (texts that aim to reach large numbers, e.g. newspapers, television)
- multimedia (the combination of two or more media in the one text—e.g., a CD–ROM might combine visual images, words, sound and film media).

We choose our language depending on the mode or medium of communication. If we don't choose appropriately, we don't communicate very well.

In a speech, for example, we generally use language differently from the way we would in a written report.

When giving a speech, we know that the audience has much less time and opportunity to take in the content than if they were reading about it. So we break the information up, use short sentences, and repeat things to help the audience follow what we are saying.

If we don't do this and instead use very long words and sentences, and pack in lots of detailed information, we overload the audience, and then lose them.

As another example, think of the way we write mobile phone text messages compared to the way we write letters or emails. In text messages, content is very, very basic and we use abbreviations and symbols to keep it as short as possible. This is to fit the message into the space allowed and to save time when sending it.

When you are considering the effect of the mode of communication in responding to a text, you need to ask two important questions:

- *How does the mode influence the text?*
- *How effective is the text for the mode?*

CHAPTER 3

Talking about language

When you comment on the **language** that composers use in their texts, you will generally have to:

- explain why it has been used, for example how it helps to achieve the text purpose
- evaluate how appropriate it is
- give examples (including quotes) to support your comments.

This chapter provides you with some ways to talk about language. We begin with some general questions that link language and context. We then look at three important language areas:

- formal or informal language
- subjective or objective language
- personal or impersonal language.

Finally we look at some language terms that will help you to be precise when talking about language.

Language techniques used in special kinds of texts are explained in **chapters 5 to 11**.

Language and context

Asking the questions below will help you explore how the language in a text reflects the context. (The pages that follow will help you answer the questions.)

- *What kind of language does the composer use?*
- *Why did he or she choose this kind of language?*
- *What other kinds of language could have been used?*
- *What effect does the language have on me?*
- *What effect would it have on the intended audience?*
- *How does the composer use language to target a particular audience?*
- *How does the language help the composer to achieve their purpose?*
- *Does the language tell you anything about any other purposes that the composer might have?*
- *How does the language reflect the society and culture in which the text was created?*
- *How would the language be different if it was created in a different time or place?*
- *What does the language tell you about the composer's values and attitudes?*
- *How well does the language suit the medium of communication?*

Formal and informal language

Formal language is language that is correct and conventional. It is the kind of language you would use in an essay or report.

Informal language or **colloquial language** is language that you would use in everyday conversation with your family and friends. It may, however, be perfectly correct grammatically.

The term **register** is often used to talk about levels of **formality** or **informality**.

Compare these:

- *You are required to present yourself at reception at 10 am.* (formal register)
- *Turn up at reception around 10 and let somebody know you're there.* (informal register)

Which sentence would be more likely in an official letter? Which would be more likely in a phone conversation?

Formal language is more common in **writing** than in **speaking**. This register is appropriate when the writer doesn't know the reader or readers. Examples of texts that are generally formal are reports, essays, newspaper reports, textbooks, and business letters.

Some language features that make a text more formal are:

- use of words that are considered standard (correct in all social groups)

- talking about things in an abstract, indirect way (e.g. *Refreshments will be served* instead of *We'll give you something to eat and drink*)
- passive voice instead of active voice (e.g. *The topic was discussed* instead of *They discussed the topic*)
- very little or no mention of composer, audience or other people (impersonal language: see **pages 42–5**).

See definitions of **abstract** language (**page 46**), and **passive voice** and **active voice** (**page 58**).

Formal language might be used sometimes because it is considered more polite and respectful, for example in letters to older people or people in authority, or in texts written in connection with important occasions or ceremonies such as funerals and weddings.

Generally texts are becoming less formal. For example, 75 years ago a newspaper journalist wrote this sentence in an article:

There are two factors to be taken into consideration when considering ways and means of combating an excessive petrol consumption—mechanical condition and driving methods.

'Combating that excessive petrol consumption', *The Cumberland Argus*, 26 October 1938.

Today, a journalist might write something like this:

> If you want to keep your petrol costs down, you need to look at how well you take care of your car and the way you drive.

Even though formal language is correct, it is not always **appropriate**. It can sound very cold and distant, and make the listener or reader feel negative about the writer or the topic.

Very formal language can also confuse or bore readers or even make them angry. Imagine, for example, that you enter an art competition and receive a letter back with these words:

> Thank you for your entry for the YouthArt Competition, received on June 10th. Your artwork was not successful on this occasion.

How would you feel? A little upset perhaps, after all your hard work? Now imagine you receive this letter instead:

> Thank you for your terrific entry in the YouthArt Competition. We really liked your work 'Flight', but we're sorry to say it was not successful this time. We very much hope you will try again next year.

How would you feel? A bit better about not winning, because of the less formal, more personal touch?

Informal or colloquial language, as already mentioned, is the language that you use in **everyday communication**. It is a more relaxed, casual way of speaking or writing, but this does not necessarily mean it is incorrect in any way.

The particular words and sentence structures used in the colloquial register are called **colloquialisms**. For example,

Hiya. What's up?
Gee, I bet he was sorry.
I reckon that's OK.
Give us a look.

Some features that make language less formal are:

- use of words and grammar patterns not considered standard, for example slang (see **pages 36–7**)
- talking about things in a direct, concrete way rather than in an abstract, indirect way (see **pages 46** and **48**)
- active voice (see **page 58**)
- frequent mention of composer, audience and other people (personal language: see **pages 42–5**).

Colloquial language is sometimes used in formal texts—for example, because a colloquial word is the best word to express a concept. The colloquial term is often put in inverted commas to show that the writer is aware of this special use. Look at these examples from school essays:

> Some boys feel it is just not 'macho' to do well in expressive subjects such as English.
>
> The death penalty is simply a 'cop out' for dealing with our social problems.

Colloquial language can sometimes be inappropriate for the context—as can formal language. Imagine you rang up about a part-time sales job and said:

> Hey man, just wanted to check out that job you advertised. Sounds mad.

Do you think you would get the job? Probably not. You assumed a close, friendly relationship with the other person that did not exist and so used colloquial language, including slang, which was not appropriate for the situation.

Slang is a form of colloquial language. It refers to words and sentence patterns that are generally only considered acceptable in very informal situations with people you know well. It is not usually regarded as acceptable in formal or semi-formal situations, such as in applying for a job.

Slang might be used by one social group only or by many social groups. These words and patterns are used mainly by young people:

Sick.
Wicked!
I was like 'hang on'.
It sucks.
And she goes 'I don't believe it'.

Many words that we now use in standard English used to be slang in past generations. For example, *bus* used to be slang for *omnibus*. Now it is the only word we use for this kind of transport.

Slang also includes words considered vulgar. **See pages 58–9.**

Some texts combine both formal and informal registers. For example, newspaper, magazine and website articles very often combine the two registers. This is usually because the purpose of the articles is to both inform and entertain. Look at this example from a website film review of *The Lord of the Rings*:

When you turn a book into a movie, things get lost. This is no exception. But the book is like a zillion pages long and the movie clocks in at over 3 hours—trust me, your favourite scene from the book may be missing, but there's plenty of stuff in this baby for all to enjoy.

When responding to a text, ask yourself:

- *Is the language register formal or informal overall?*
- *Are there parts of the text that go against the overall pattern?*
- *Is there a combination of registers? If so, why?*
- *How appropriate is this kind of language to the context?*
- *If formal language is used, does it make the text more difficult to understand? Does it become cold and uninteresting? Does it insult or offend?*
- *If informal varieties of language are used, does it make the text realistic and convincing?*
- *Is slang used that only one group might understand? Why does the composer do this?*
- *Is slang used to get the audience onside with the composer's ideas? Does this work?*
- *Would any language be offensive to some of the audience? How would this affect their response to the text?*

Remember: Give examples (including quotes) to support your comments.

Subjective and objective language

Subjective (or evaluative) language indicates an attitude to, or feeling about, the topic.

Objective language does not show any attitude or feeling. It is focused on facts and information only.

For example:

> Sadly, the group's valiant attempts to save the whale were in vain.
>
> The group's attempts to save the whale were not successful.

Which one shows what the writer thought about the group and the whale?

In the first sentence, the words *sadly*, *valiant* and *in vain* indicate that the writer was on the side of the group wanting to save the whale. In the second sentence, the writer keeps this view out of the sentence and just reports the facts.

Some subjective language is called **emotive**, because it is designed to make the audience respond emotionally to what is being written or spoken about.

For example:

> The decision has devastated the whole community.
>
> The decision is opposed by the whole community.

In the first sentence, *devastated* is an emotive word. (We immediately think of people's experiences and feelings in earthquakes and other terrible events.) In the second sentence, *is opposed* is a more factual, objective way of saying that the decision was not popular.

Subjective language is used all the time in literary texts where the composer's purpose is to openly express personal attitudes and feelings. It is expected that novelists or poets, for example, will use subjective language.

However, in factual texts, where the purpose generally is to give information, composers have a choice. They can present information in a subjective or objective way.

Let's look at this sentence from a feature article:

> Hundreds of health freaks filled the large auditorium, desperate to hear about the latest fad diet.

The words *health freaks*, *desperate* and *fad* are all subjective. They reflect the writer's negative view of people who are so interested in health that they attend lectures about it. However, there is no way to be sure that the people are truly *health freaks* (whatever that might mean), that they are *desperate*, or that the new diet is a *fad* that will last only a few months.

If the writer was being completely objective they would have written the sentence like this:

> Hundreds of people filled the auditorium to hear about the new diet.

Many factual texts include both subjective and objective language.

> Understanding subjective and objective language is an important part of critically responding to texts. See **chapter 4**.

When responding to a text, ask yourself:

- *Is the language subjective or objective overall?*
- *Are there parts of the text that go against the overall pattern?*
- *How appropriate is this kind of language to the context?*
- *If the language is subjective, what does it tell you about the composer's attitudes or feelings on the topic?*

  How does the subjective language affect your confidence in any factual information in the text?
- *Does the subjective language make you positive or negative about the composer's attitudes or feelings?*
- *If objective language is used, how does this affect your belief in the information or views in the text?*

- *Does the objective language make you positive or negative about the composer's attitudes or feelings on the topic?*

Remember: Give examples (including quotes) to support your comments.

Personal and impersonal language

Personal language creates a personal connection between the composer and the audience. This personal relationship is an important focus of the text.

Impersonal language does not make any personal connection with the audience. The focus is totally on the topic of the text.

We sometimes call this aspect of language the **tone**—either a personal or an impersonal tone.

We usually use a personal tone when we communicate with people we know well. However, we often use a personal tone with people we do not know well—for example, to capture and then hold the audience's attention, and to persuade the audience.

Look at these examples:

- *I ask you now, friends, to think about this.* (speech)
- *Let's get together to tackle this problem now.* (letter to the editor)

- *Now consider if you will, dear reader, how young Dorothea might have reacted to this news.* (novel)
- *If you have ever wondered what heaven is like ...* (advertisement for ice cream)

Some language techniques that make a text more personal are:

- talking directly to the reader or listener using *you*, that is, using the **second person** form
- talking as if the composer and audience are part of the same group (e.g. *let's*, *we all*, *if we* and *now we can see*) using the **first person plural** form (often called **inclusive language**)
- using the **active voice** instead of the **passive voice**, e.g. *The community is asking questions*, instead of *Questions are being asked by the community*
- asking **rhetorical questions** (questions you don't expect the audience to answer, e.g. *So what can we conclude from this?*)
- using colloquial language to talk about the topic.

Advertisers, for example, often adopt a personal tone even though they do not know the audience. They do this to attract the audience and to establish a friendly, positive attitude towards the product being advertised.

Look at these examples from advertisements:

- *Thought I would let you in on a little secret…*
- *None of us like to feel we are spending money for nothing…*
- *Psst! When was the last time you...*

Impersonal language does not make any personal connection with the audience. The focus is totally on the topic. We generally use an impersonal tone when we communicate with people we do not know well or at all, especially when writing—for example, in essays, instructions and reports.

For example:

- *Galaxies are classified according to their shape.* (report)
- *The man was arrested shortly after dawn.* (newspaper report)
- *Youth services are a major issue.* (feature article)

Some language techniques that make a text impersonal are:

- using the passive voice instead of the active, for example *Galaxies are classified* instead of *We classify galaxies…*
- narrating in the **third person** (*he, she, it, they*) instead of the first person (*I, we*) and second person (*you*)

- mentioning things and processes rather than people
- using formal language to talk about the topic.

Writers sometimes get the tone wrong for their audience and purpose. Look back at the YouthArt Competition letter on **page 34**. The writer of the first letter used an inappropriate tone. The writer employed very impersonal language when a more personal tone would have been better suited to the situation.

When responding to a text, you should ask yourself:

- *Is the language personal or impersonal overall?*
- *Are there parts of the text that go against the overall pattern?*
- *What language techniques does the composer use to make it personal or impersonal?*
- *Why has the composer used this kind of language? For example, has the composer used personal language to get the audience's attention? To make them agree with his or her view?*
- *Has the composer used impersonal language to keep the reader's focus on the information?*
- *Would the text be more effective if it were more personal or more impersonal?*

Remember: Give examples (including quotes) from the text to support your comments.

Other important language terms and concepts

The following language terms will help you to be precise when talking or writing about the language used in texts. You will find more language terms relevant to particular types of texts in the chapters on those texts (**chapters 5 to 11**).

Abstract language is language that refers to things in a distant, generalised way. Look at these two sentences:

- *Screen violence can have a negative influence on the behaviour of children.*
- *When children see people saying and doing violent things to each other on television and film, it can make them behave badly themselves.*

The first sentence is more abstract than the second. It does not talk about things in real, concrete terms.

Abstract language is more common in formal texts such as essays and reports.

Heavy use of abstract language can make a text seem very formal, dense and difficult to read. See **concrete** language, **page 48**.

Acronyms are words formed from the initial letters of a group of words. They are a type of abbreviation. For example AIDS for Acquired Immune Deficiency Syndrome, or ASH for Action on Smoking and Health.

Active voice. See **voice, page 58**.

Ambiguity occurs when a word or group of words has more than one meaning—we say that the word or group of words is **ambiguous.** For example the sentence *I asked you to do it quietly* can be interpreted as either *I spoke quietly when I asked you to do it* or *I wanted you to do it in a quiet manner.*

Antonyms are opposite words. *Black* is the antonym of *white.*

Archaic language is language that is from an earlier time and no longer used in ordinary speech. Archaic language may sometimes be borrowed for use in modern times. For example: *ye* for *the*; *thou* for *you*; *sayest* for *say.*

Clichés are overused expressions. Because they are overused, they do not have much meaning any more. They can give the impression that the speaker or writer does not have original ideas. Examples are:

If you can't beat them, join them
All's well that ends well
Last, but not least

Many idioms become clichés. See **idiomatic language, page 51**.

Coherence refers to whether or not a text makes sense. A **coherent** text makes sense. An **incoherent** text does not.

Cohesion refers to the way a text 'hangs together' as one whole thing. If you read a text and it seems to flow easily from one sentence to the next, and from one paragraph to the next, then it is **cohesive**. Certain language devices help us make our texts cohesive—for example, **connectives** such as *therefore*, *in addition*, *secondly*. (See **page 157**.)

Collocation refers to the way certain words commonly occur together or in certain order. For example, we say *crystal clear* but we don't say *glass clear*. We say *fluent English* but not *easy* or *free-flowing English*. We say *bread and butter* not *butter and bread*.

Concrete language is language that describes actual, real and particular objects and ideas—the opposite of **abstract**. For example, the sentence *People in the city live closer to one another than they do in the country* is more concrete than *Population density is greater in urban areas*. See also **abstract**, **page 46**.

Connotation refers to the ideas or feelings that are suggested by a word. For example, for many people the word *lady* has connotations of femininity and proper behaviour that the word *woman* does not.

Dialect is the particular language of a group of people, usually from the same part of a country. It is more than a strong accent—people who speak a dialect use different grammar and a different vocabulary from people in other parts of their country. Dialects usually have their own slang forms. In fact, groups that make extreme use of slang (for example street gangs) are sometimes considered to be using a dialect. Parents sometimes joke that their teenagers speak a kind of dialect, because they can't understand the slang that their children use.

Direct speech refers to reporting of words from actual conversations in a text. When direct speech is used in a written text, quotation marks ("...") are used: *Jones said, "I have to leave."* **Indirect** (or **reported**) speech occurs when the writer or speaker reports what another person has said but the exact words are not used: *Jones said that he had to leave.*

Ellipsis is the omission of words that repeat what has been said already, e.g. *Josie and Sonia arrived late in the afternoon and quickly began work.* We don't repeat *Josie and Sonia* after *and* because it is clear they are the ones who quickly began work. The ellipsis makes the sentence easier to read.
Note: Ellipsis also refers to the three dot points used to indicate missing words or a pause in a text (...).

Emotive language. See **pages 39** and **125–6**.

Euphemisms are words that are used in preference to more accurate but less polite or pleasant alternatives—for example, *passed away* instead of *dying*, *washroom* instead of *toilet*. Most euphemisms are harmless but some are coined to 'cover over' (and depersonalise) very serious concepts or events. For example, there are many euphemisms for the consequences of war, such as *collateral damage* instead of *accidental killing of civilians.*

Expletives are exclamations, usually impolite ones, such as *damn*. These days the word mostly refers to the more offensive 'four-letter' swear words. See also **vulgar language**, **pages 58–9**.

Figurative language refers to words and expressions that do not mean exactly what they say. We can also call such language **metaphorical**. Figurative language is not meant to be read literally. For example, if you said *the jury is still out*, you wouldn't exactly mean that a jury had been formed to decide an issue. You simply mean that the various people involved have not come to a decision yet. The expression *the jury is still out* is a **figure of speech** as it does not rely on making literal sense for its meaning. See also **idiomatic language**, **page 51** and **literal meaning**, **page 52**.

Fillers are expressions like *um, er, ah, okay, right, like.* They are used to *fill in* while you think of what to say, or sometimes to make your language more personal or colloquial.

Formal language. See **pages 32–8**.

Hyperbole is the use of exaggeration for a particular effect. It is not meant to be taken literally. For example, if your best friend says *I will kill you if you do that*, they do not mean that they will actually kill you. They are simply using a particular means of expression to encourage you to do what they want. Hyperbole is a variety of **figurative language**.

Idiomatic language is an everyday use of **figurative language**. An **idiom** is a group of words that has a different meaning from what it would have if each word were taken separately. For example, the expressions *drop a bombshell* and *there are plenty more fish in the sea* would be understood by most English speakers to mean 'say something shocking' and 'there will be other people to fall in love with'. However, a person who is learning English as their second language might have difficulty understanding the sentence *The Prime Minister dropped a bombshell*. We use idioms more commonly in everyday conversation than in other contexts.

Imperative is a grammatical term referring to verbs being used as commands or instructions. In the sentences *Listen to me*, *Turn the switch to the right* and *Go if you want to*, the underlined words are imperative verbs.

Impersonal language. See **pages 42–5**.

Informal language. See **pages 32–8**.

Interrogative is a grammatical term referring to words and sentence patterns that form questions. Some interrogative structures are clearly questions—*Who* *are you?* and *Are you going?*—while others depend on **intonation** (see below)—*You like me?*

Intonation refers to the rising and falling patterns of speech. Our intonation usually rises at the end of a question and falls at the end of a sentence. Intonation can also alter the meaning of a sentence, for example, by expressing attitude (*I think so*—rising intonation expressing doubt).

Jargon is the technical language of a particular field (see also **technical language, page 56**). Jargon is fine to use when you know the audience will understand it. If this is not the case, using jargon can be insulting and offensive. The audience may also think that the writer or speaker is trying to impress them, and this can make them doubt the truth of their words. Examples of jargon from the field of tennis are *drop shot*, *volley* and *deuce*. Technical fields such as computer science abound in jargon.

Literal meaning is the natural or strict meaning of a word or phrase. The literal meaning of *to grasp an idea* would be 'to hold an idea in your hands'. Of course, it does not mean this. It means 'to understand an idea'. This is its **figurative** or **metaphoric** meaning (see **figurative language page 50**). Literal language is preferred for formal texts such as reports and technical manuals as it is generally clearer.

Metaphor (or **metaphorical language**). See **page 90**.

Modality is the use of certain words and phrases to show how we feel about an idea—generally how certain we are or how strongly we feel. Examples are *definitely, absolutely, perhaps, it's possible* and *to an extent.* **Modal verbs** are small verbs like *must, can, have to, could, might and ought to* which help us to express these concepts.

Nominalisation is the process of making nouns and noun phrases from verbs, for example, *treatment* from *treat, achievement* from *achieve, excessive water wastage* from *they wasted a lot of water.* We frequently use nominalisations in formal and abstract writing to keep it impersonal and to help 'pack in' information.

Non-verbal communication is communication that does not involve words. It is generally used to refer to **body language**—facial expressions, hand gestures, body movements and positions. For example, raising your eyebrows is a facial gesture that, in English-speaking cultures, can mean you are surprised by what the other person has said.

Objective language. See **page 70**.

Obsolete language is language that is no longer used. For example, the word *horologe* is an obsolete word meaning a watch, clock or other timepiece.

Oxymoron is a combination of two words or phrases that are opposite or contradictory to emphasise your meaning—for example, *a weak tyrant, a hateful love.*

Passive voice. See **voice, page 58**.

Person is a grammatical term that refers to three types of address within a text: **first person**—the speaker or writer (*I*, *we*, *me*, *us*); **second person**—the person spoken or written to (*you*); or **third person**—anyone (or anything) else (*he*, *she*, *it*, *they*). Using the first and second person in a text can be more direct and personal than using the third person.

Personal language. See **pages 42–5**.

Prose is written language in ordinary form (that is, sentences and paragraphs). We usually talk of prose when we want to distinguish this kind of writing from **poetic** writing.

Redundant words are unnecessary words. For example, in the sentence *He is a bad evil man*, the word *bad* is redundant because *evil* means *very bad*. See also **tautology, page 56**.

Register is a reference to how formal or informal the language is. See **formal** and **informal language, page 32**.

Rhetorical questions are questions asked for a special effect, for example to involve the audience personally. The questioner does not expect answers to these questions—for example, *So why do we all want to believe in aliens?* (from a speech). Rhetorical questions are often used to persuade the audience to accept a particular point of view. See also **page 43**.

Sexist language is language that displays a negative attitude towards one sex or another. Usually this negative attitude is expressed towards females. The writer or speaker does not always mean to insult women—sexist language is often used out of tradition or convention. For example, it has been common for hundreds of years to talk of *man* or *mankind* to mean all humans. Whether intended or not, sexist language suggests that women are less important. Good composers do their best to employ **non-sexist** or **gender-neutral** language in their texts.

One common example of sexist language is the use of *he* to mean people in general, for example:
The teacher should always encourage his students to think for themselves.

A **non-sexist** way to write this would be:
The teacher should always encourage his or her students to think for themselves.

Or, you could make the sentence plural and write:
Teachers should always encourage their students to think for themselves. (This is often the simplest way to solve this problem.)

Simile. See **page 93**.

Slogan is a brief expression that is used to promote a message. Slogans are often used by political parties, advertisers, community safety groups and other activists —for example, *This Time One Nation* (to promote a political party), *Belt Up* (to promote seat-belt use), *Slip Slop Slap* (to encourage skin protection).

Subjective language. See **pages 39–42**.

Synonyms are words that have the same (or a similar) meaning. For example, *thin* and *skinny* are **synonymous** terms.

Tautology is unnecessary repetition. For example, in the sentence *Can you repeat that statement again?* the word *again* is not needed because *repeat* means *to do again*. We say that the word *again* is **redundant** and the sentence *Can you repeat that statement again?* is **tautological**.

Technical language is language used to refer to specialised areas of knowledge. For example, in the field of computers, the words *byte*, *hard drive*, *cookie* and *compiler* are technical terms. Technical language is often necessary to talk about a special area of knowledge. However, if the audience does not know the language, they can feel excluded and even offended by its use. Technical language used inappropriately is usually called **jargon**.

Tense refers to the form of a verb which describes the time that the action takes place. The three main tenses are present tense (*run*), past tense (*ran*) and future tense (*will run*). We choose a particular tense form to be clear about when things happened. Sometimes, however, we choose a tense for a particular effect. For example, we might use the present tense instead of the past to make a narrative more immediate for the reader. Read more about tense in **chapter 13**.

Tone refers to the attitude or feeling of the composer that comes through in the text. A tone might be humorous, light-hearted, serious, sarcastic, authoritative, respectful, and so on. Tone is also used to talk about **personal** or **impersonal language** (see **pages 44–5**).

Topic sentence is the sentence in a paragraph that states the main idea. It is usually the first sentence.

Verbose style refers to using many words where only a few would do. For example, *at this point in time* can normally be shortened to *now*.

Vogue words are words that are in fashion for a while. They might be idiomatic or slang but not necessarily. Recent examples are *bottom line*, *touch base* and *absolutely*. Use of these words can suggest that the speaker or writer is just trying to impress, or that they cannot think of better ways to say what they mean.

There is also the problem that they often go quickly out of fashion, and then become **clichés**.

Voice, in the grammatical sense, refers to whether a sentence is **active** or **passive**. The sentence *Gina won the race* is in the active voice while the sentence *The race was won by Gina* is in the passive voice.

We usually use the **active voice** when we are interested in the people we are talking or writing about. We often use the **passive voice** in formal writing, such as essays and reports, because we are more interested in processes and actions than in the people involved. For example:

Ten subjects were interviewed. Their answers were recorded on videotape.

Voice may also refer to the sense of person that comes through the composer's words. For example, John Marsden's series *Tomorrow, When The War Began* is written from the perspective and with the voice of a teenage girl.

Vulgar language is language that is both unacceptable and offensive to many people. Vulgar language usually refers to sex or bodily functions. It includes 'four-letter' swear words. People differ in their views of what is vulgar language and what is not. People also differ in their views of when vulgar language might be acceptable and when it might not.

Vulgar language becomes a problem when two people communicating have different ideas about what is acceptable. For example, your 90-year-old great-grandmother might have different ideas from you about what is vulgar.

Remember: There are more language terms in **chapters 5 to 11**.

CHAPTER 4

Critically responding to texts

At some point in your English studies you will be asked to look at texts in a **critical** way. This chapter helps you understand what the critical approach is about. It gives you some strategies to use, explains some important terms and concepts, and includes questions and examples to help you.

What does 'critically responding' mean?

Every text is composed by a living, breathing person. This person has had many personal, social and cultural experiences, and has developed values, and attitudes to people, places and events, based on these experiences.

This means that the person will have an attitude to the text topic, and to the people, places and events mentioned in the text. He or she will also have a particular purpose for composing a text on that topic, and for talking about those people, places or events.

With some texts, it can be difficult to work out the composer's values, attitudes and purpose, because they may be quite hidden. However, values, attitude and purpose usually do come through in the choice of topic, and in the language used to talk about the people, places and events in the text. They also come through in the choice of visual images used. This is what **critically responding** is all about.

Critically responding to a text does not mean trying to find fault with it. It means looking at the topic and at the language used to talk about the people, places and events, and asking:

- *Why did the composer talk about these people, places and events in this way?*
- *What other ways could the composer have talked about them? How might a different composer have talked about them?*
- *What is the composer's attitude to the people, places or events?*
- *What does the composer want me think or feel about them?*

Critically responding involves not simply accepting everything you read or hear as true, reliable or reasonable. Composers might, for example,

- leave out important facts and information, or express them in a way to suit their own views

- express opinions that are biased or illogical
- express opinions in a way that makes them sound like fact
- use language techniques and visual images that influence the audience to think or feel as they do on the topic.

It is very important when reading any text to keep a critical perspective. There are few truly neutral texts—that is, texts that are completely objective. Even fact sheets, information websites and textbooks may reflect the composer's personal values or assumptions. Remember that a text may seek to influence you by selecting some facts and leaving out other facts that may well be relevant.

Responding critically is necessary for both literary texts and factual texts. In novels and films, for example, the writers or film-makers appear to be simply telling a story, but they have made choices about what stories to tell, and what characters, situations and plotlines to use. You need to think about what these choices say about the composer's values and attitudes.

When responding critically to a text you should think about the kinds of things covered in **chapter 2**. In particular, you should think about purpose, audience and the identity of the composer.

Look at this short extract from a website about the International Space Station.

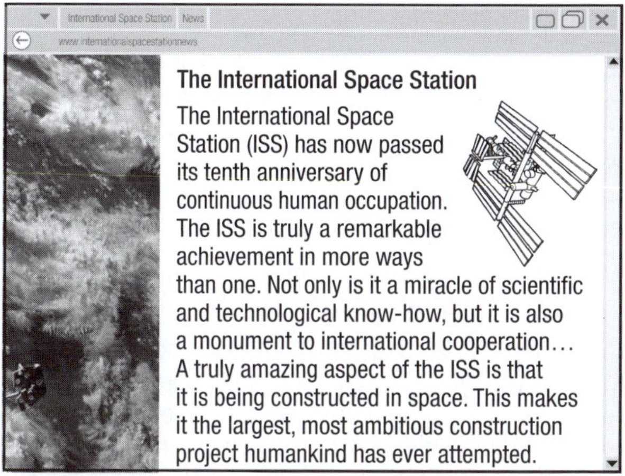

The International Space Station

The International Space Station (ISS) has now passed its tenth anniversary of continuous human occupation. The ISS is truly a remarkable achievement in more ways than one. Not only is it a miracle of scientific and technological know-how, but it is also a monument to international cooperation… A truly amazing aspect of the ISS is that it is being constructed in space. This makes it the largest, most ambitious construction project humankind has ever attempted.

If we apply the four questions on **page 61** to this short extract we might make these comments:

- *Why did the composer talk about these people, places and events in this way?*

It looks like the writer just wants to inform us about the ISS. But if we ask why, we might guess that she or he wants to encourage a positive attitude towards it. There has been a lot of negative talk about the ISS, especially since the Columbia disaster in 2003, in which seven people died.

- *What other ways could the composer have talked about them? How might a different composer have talked about them?*

Another writer might have focused instead on the expenses and dangers. For example, a newspaper report after the Columbia disaster said that the ISS was a huge waste of money, and reported that the government of the United States was very nervous about rising costs.

- *What is the composer's attitude to the people, places or events?*

The writer has a positive attitude to the ISS, and to space exploration in general (again, something some people are negative about). The choice of language tells us this (*remarkable achievement, miracle of scientific and technological know-how, truly amazing*).

- *What does the composer want me think or feel about them?*

The writer wants us to think positively towards the ISS. The more the world is interested in it, the harder it will be to stop the ISS program.

When making critical comments like these, you should support them with evidence from the text wherever possible.

Some strategies for factual texts

These strategies will help you respond critically to factual texts, in particular:

- Take notice of who the composer is. *Is the composer an expert? An ordinary member of the community? A journalist? A member of an organisation which supports a particular view?*
- Think about how the composer's identity might influence what he or she has said.
- Be especially careful when reading information from websites. People need no special qualification or knowledge to establish a website.
- Be wary of any texts where the author's name is not given (an exception is newspaper editorials, where the view expressed is the official view of the editors).
- Be careful to distinguish between fact and opinion. Be on the lookout for opinion disguised as fact—for example: *Most people believe that… It has been alleged that … Mr Smith is understood to be …*
- Pay close attention to words that show the writer's attitude towards a topic, for example *unfortunately, fortunately, disastrous, embarrassing, humiliating.*
- Think about why a certain word has been used to describe people, places or events, and how the

choice of this word may affect the view of the intended audience. For example, if you read about *noisy protesters* in a newspaper report, you might be inclined to think differently about them than if you had just read *protesters*.

- Remember that some words have positive or negative connotations. For example, a reader might think differently about people described as *greenies* and people described as *environmentalists*. For many people, the first word has negative connotations that the second word does not and vice versa.
- Think about other ways in which the topics could have been talked about. For example, if the *noisy protesters* were actually workers protesting about being sacked without notice, they might also be described as *sacked workers*. If so, you might feel much more sympathetically towards them.
- Think about the use of any visual images. *Why have the particular images been used? How do they affect your response?*
- Think about your own view on the topic, and whether you accept the composer's view.

There is more about the use of visual images in **chapter 9**.

Important 'critical' terms and concepts

The following terms will help you to talk or write critically about a text. For many terms, there are questions to help you know what to look for in texts.

Bias is where a text favours one view without giving sufficient reason for that view, or only gives one set of facts and arguments, and ignores facts and arguments on the other side. The text composer's bias may come through the use of **stereotypes** (see **pages 72–3**) and **subjective** language (see **pages 39–42**).

You should ask yourself:

- *Does the composer present only one side of the issue or events?*
- *Does the composer give <u>any</u> facts or arguments to support his or her view?*
- *Does the composer <u>only</u> use facts or arguments that support his or her view?*
- *Does the composer ignore facts or arguments on the other side?*

It is sometimes acceptable to present one point of view, for example, in a letter to the editor or an essay. But a point of view will always be more persuasive if it is supported with facts and/or good reasons. It will also be more persuasive if it recognises arguments on the other side. (Remember this in your own writing and speaking.)

Culture is the way of life of a group of people—everything they say, do, believe and value in their lives. All texts reflect, in some way, the culture in which they were composed. Many aspects of culture are passed down from generation to generation. However, some aspects of culture may change over time. Ask yourself: *How has the cultural background of the text influenced what is in the text?* See also **Social and cultural context**, **pages 25–7**.

Cultural assumptions are beliefs or feelings that are 'taken for granted' in a society (in other words, not often questioned). They are usually about gender, age, ethnicity, work, education or social class. These assumptions often come through in texts.

One common kind of cultural assumption is about **gender**. Sometimes writers appear to assume that males are more important than females. One way this comes through in a text is by the use of male pronouns (*he, him, his*) to talk in general about people or about the audience. **Gender assumptions** may also come through in fiction texts in the roles given to males and females—for example, the strong, interesting central characters always being male and the weak, less interesting ones being female.

These assumptions reflect the traditional roles of males and females in society, but in today's world are not accurate or fair.

Another kind of cultural assumption is about race and ethnicity. For example, a newspaper article may show through the language used to describe certain social groups that the writer assumes all the readers are white and of Anglo-Celtic background.

You should ask yourself:

- *Does the composer assume certain things about a group in our society, and if so are these assumptions valid?*
- *Does the composer assume everyone is from the same cultural group as she or he is?*
- *Does the composer assume that the audience has the same attitude to this cultural group as she or he does?*

Gender roles are the way male and female roles are presented in a text. Males, for example, might occupy all the strong leading roles in a fiction text; or males might be presented as a bit stupid and hopeless, as in many television advertisements these days. Females in advertisements might be presented as sex objects, or as homemakers who care only about clean bench-tops.

Ask yourself:

- *What do the roles given to men and women in the text say about their roles in society?*
- *Are the gender roles stereotypical?* (See **stereotype**, **pages 72–3**.)

- *Is one gender omitted from the text altogether?*
- *Are the strong roles mainly given to one gender?*
- *Is the composer trying to influence the way the audience sees gender roles? Why?*

Objective language is used to express ideas and information in a factual way. The composer's view is not mentioned or hinted at. It is the opposite of **subjective**.

You should look at **pages 38–41** for a full explanation of subjective and objective language.

Perspective, orientation or position (of the composer) is the composer's view and attitude towards the text topic and the people, places and events related to the topic. See also **subjective language**, **pages 39–42**.

Ask yourself:

- *What is the composer's view or attitude to the topic of the text, and the people, places and events in the text?*
- *How does this come through in the text?*
- *What other view is possible?*
- *What is my view?*

Popular culture refers to the experiences and interests of a wide range of people in a community or society. Films often reflect popular culture. Being critical often involves questioning the popular culture.

Positioning refers to the way some texts attempt to manipulate, influence or even control the audience's view on a topic. Composers do this by choosing what they talk about and how they talk about it.

Look at this example from a newspaper column: *Everyone who cares about justice will want immediate action on this issue.*

When the reader reads this sentence they are likely to think *Well, I care about justice, so I agree with this writer—I want action now too.* This is precisely the response the writer wants.

Ask yourself:

- *Does the composer assume I have the same view as he or she does?*
- *Do I have the same view?*
- *What does the composer want me to think or feel about this topic?*
- *Are there good reasons to be or not to be influenced by the composer's view?*

Representation refers to the process of using words or images to indicate deeper meanings. For example, speed limit signs represent the fact that our society values safety on the roads. Film-makers often use images to reveal something about their characters that would be difficult to reveal using dialogue. For example, the director might film a character looking at themself in a broken mirror to indicate that the character has a split personality.

Society is a group of people who live together in the same place (e.g. same country) and who share a way of life and culture. All texts reflect in some way the society in which they are created. See also **social and cultural context, pages 25–7**.

Stereotype is a fixed set of ideas and cultural assumptions about a particular type or group of people or things—ideas that are wrongly believed to be shared by all people or things of this type or group.

Stereotypes can be about, for example, social background, ethnic background, religious beliefs, gender, age, place of living, type of work, school and interests.

Stereotypes can be very offensive, especially if you belong to one of the groups being stereotyped. However, they are not always offensive. In cartoons, for example, stereotypes are very useful to quickly establish a character's background and attitude.

Stereotypes are often used for humorous or dramatic purposes. In film and television, for example, these stereotypes are common:

- *Blonde women are not very smart.*
- *People interested in computers are social outcasts.*
- *People who wear glasses are clever.*

Ask yourself:

- *Are some characters stereotypical? In what ways?*
- *Is the stereotype offensive to the intended audience or to you?*
- *Does the stereotype serve a useful purpose for the composer? What purpose?*
- *Does the stereotype encourage a certain attitude towards the social group it represents?*

Values are what we consider good, important and desirable in life. In general, people of different cultures value the same kinds of things. For example, in the Australian culture most people value money (as well as other things). Of course, people differ in their values. For example, one person might value money more than another.

Ask yourself: *What does the choice of subject, and the way it is referred to, tell you about the composer's values?*

CHAPTER 5

Responding to written fiction

Written fiction includes novels, short stories and traditional fiction such as fables and legends. Written fiction is mostly **narrative**. That is, it aims to tell a story—usually to entertain, to amuse or to help us make sense of events and experiences that affect our lives.

When responding to written fiction—either whole texts or extracts—you will generally make comment on these broad areas:

- plot
- setting
- structure
- character
- theme
- language and style.

These six areas overlap very much, and it can be difficult to talk about one without referring to another. For example, you will need to refer to characters when you talk about the plot.

Nevertheless, it is useful to think about each area in turn and to use these areas to organise your ideas when responding.

The following section explains what is covered by each of these six areas. It also includes other terms and concepts you will need to understand. You will not always need to comment on *all* of these things when responding to a text—that will depend on the task your teacher sets.

Use the list of terms as a checklist. Ask yourself: *Should I comment on this aspect of the narrative?*

1 Your teacher may ask you to comment on the way language is used in a narrative text, for example, to create the atmosphere. You will need to use some of the terms in **chapter 4** to do this.

2 Many of the terms that follow are also relevant to stage or film. See **chapters 7 and 8**.

Important terms and concepts

Appropriation occurs when something is taken from one text and used in a different way in another text. The **appropriated** feature might be a character, the style of the text or the plotline. For example, in his comical fantasy book *Truckers*, Terry Pratchett appropriates the style of the Old Testament to relate the origins of the imaginary Nome tribe. He begins each chapter with excerpts from *The Book of Nome*, and uses expressions such as *In the beginning; Let there be* and *Thus it was*.

Atmosphere refers to the feeling or **mood** created by a text. The atmosphere may be evoked by a particular setting or scene or by the whole narrative. The atmosphere could be gloomy, depressing, hopeful, threatening, suspenseful or calm.

Bathos. See **page 81**.

Characters are the people who are involved in the events of the story. Sometimes, of course, the characters might not be human—they might be animals, robots or imaginary creatures.

You can divide the characters into **major** and **minor** character groups. You might identify a **hero** (male) or a **heroine** (female). These are the most important characters in the narrative—usually the ones who do good things or receive our sympathy for some reason (see also **protagonist** and **antagonist**, **page 82**).

You might also identify an **anti-hero**—a character who would normally be classified as a hero but who lacks the usual positive characteristics and virtues. Bart Simpson in the television show *The Simpsons* is a good example of an anti-hero.

Character traits. As well as identifying the characters, you will need to talk about what they are like as people and give evidence to support your view. You might talk about the following dimensions of character:

- strong or weak
- morally good or bad
- mean or kind-hearted
- extroverted or introverted
- anxious or carefree
- popular or unpopular
- warm or cold
- aggressive or timid
- confident or not confident.

You might also talk about how realistic the characters are, that is, how closely they resemble real people. Characters can be described as **multi-dimensional** if they exhibit the complexity of real people. Such characters often display a complex mix of opposing character traits. They might be aggressive but kind-hearted, or extroverted but fearful. The most interesting characters are usually multi-dimensional.

Characterisation refers to the way the writer creates and develops the characters in general or individually.

Ask yourself:

- *Are the characters stereotypical or well-rounded?*

- *Do they stay the same or do they change?*
- *Are they developed through the dialogue and their actions or are we simply told about them?*
- *Do they interact with other characters, and if so, how?*
- *Are we aware of their thoughts or must we imagine what they are thinking?*
- *Do they contrast with any other characters in the text?*

Climax and **complication**. See **structure, page 83**.

Descriptive language is language used to create a picture in the reader's mind of what is being described —a scene, a character or an experience. **Adjectives** are frequently used in descriptions. For example, an old woman might be described as having ***tired old*** hands, skin ***pale*** and ***mottled***, fingers ***swollen*** and ***gnarled***.

However, descriptions may also be effective without many adjectives:

An old lady leaps from her wheelchair, waving her banner in the air as her favourite player goes crashing over the line. She can barely see the scoreboard through her inch-thick glasses, but she knows she's in front and there's not long till the full-time hooter.

You may need to comment on how important description is to the narrative, and how effective it is.

Dialogue is what the characters say to each other in the text. Strictly speaking, it refers to conversation between two people, but it is often used in a more general way to talk about conversations. Often the main way you will learn about the characters is through their dialogue. Dialogue is also used to develop the story and the theme—we find out what happened and understand its significance by reading or hearing what the characters say to each other.

Empathy describes the feeling of understanding how the characters feel and why they behave as they do. You may feel empathy when a writer describes events or occurrences that you have experienced yourself. Compare **sympathy**, **page 85**.

Episodes are the incidents or events that occur in the narrative.

Genre refers to the type of narrative. Examples of genres are fantasy, crime or detective, romance, spy, science fiction, horror, adventure and social realism. Specific genres tend to have similar topics, style, language and structure. For example, narratives in the romance genre usually involve a man meeting a woman. One falls in love with the other and meets obstacles in attempting to have the other fall in love with them, and finally they are united in love. Many narratives in the crime or detective genre feature bitter, tough-talking detectives who have problems in their personal lives.

Intertextuality is one text's relationship to another. This could be when:

- a quote, character or image from one text is used in another text (for example, an advertisement might use lines from a famous poem)
- a whole text is based on another text for its meaning (for example, Roald Dahl's *Revolting Rhymes* are a 'send up' of traditional nursery rhymes and tales)
- the whole text is an imitation of another text but set in a different time and place (for example, the film *Clueless* is a 20th century version of the 19th century Jane Austen novel *Emma*).

Narrator is the person telling the story. She or he must decide which **narrative point of view** to adopt to tell it. In many narratives, the writer tells the story as though she or he is there as an onlooker—seeing everything that happens in every scene, and knowing what everyone thinks and feels. This is called a **third person narration**.

Writing in the third person generally makes the story less personal and more objective. The audience sees the story from the perspective of all the characters, for example *Mick moved silently towards the door. Joel watched in terror.*

In other stories the writer adopts the **persona** of one of the characters to tell the story. This character tells the story from their own perspective, only relating what they can know about. This is called **first person narration**. Writing in the first person makes the story more personal. The audience feel like they are 'inside the character's head'—for example: *I moved silently towards the door. Joel watched me, terror written all over his face.*

Orientation. See **structure, pages 82–4**.

Pathos is the power of a narrative to cause the audience to feel sadness or pity because of the characters' experiences (for example, the death of a loved one). Pathos can be contrasted with **bathos**, which is a sudden and inappropriate change from something important or serious to something very ordinary or trivial. The sudden change is not always intended by the writer!

Plot or **storyline** refers to what happens in the narrative—the important events that occur at different points in the story. When responding to a literary text you will usually have to **summarise** the plot. A **plot summary** is sometimes called a **plot synopsis**.

Don't make the mistake of including too much detail.

Your teacher has read the text and does not want you to retell the whole story. However, your teacher does want to see evidence that you *know* the whole story.

A good way to become familiar with how to briefly summarise plots is to look at book jacket blurbs. However, you should *not* use these as models. Their purpose is to sell the book and so is quite different from your own purpose.

Protagonist. This is the character who drives the action of the story. The protagonist might be the hero or heroine (if the text has one) or some other character. Many stories also have an **antagonist**, a character who works in opposition to the protagonist.

Resolution. See **structure**, **pages 82–4**.

Setting refers to where and when the events take place. There may be more than one setting. You need to relate the setting to the plot and the theme. Settings may be symbolic—for example, cold, windswept landscapes may reflect the sad or mysterious events of the plot.

Structure of the narrative refers to how the story begins, how it is developed, and how it ends. Narratives have traditionally followed these **stages**:

- **orientation**—introduction to the events, characters and setting

- **complication**—the main events of the story (usually the characters' attempts to deal with conflict), leading up to the critical event or problem when conflict is at its peak (often called the **climax**)
- **resolution** or **dénouement**—the actions and speech of the characters immediately after the climax, usually dealing with the consequences of the conflict or its resolution
- **comment** or **reflection** on the events in the story (also called a **coda**)—this is sometimes a statement of the moral of the story (not always included).

You might have to identify these stages, or comment on the effectiveness of each stage. Long narratives such as novels do not have clear divisions between these stages, but many novels will follow this general pattern. Other novels play around with the pattern considerably. In fact many modern novels and short stories do not follow the traditional narrative structure.

For example, the writer may begin with the story complication (for example, a crime or the end of a relationship) and then **backtrack** to reveal how the complication came about. Or they might omit one stage altogether, or combine two or more stages. A **linear** structure is one where the plot unfolds in the same sequence as the events occur. It differs from a

retrospective structure that starts with the most recent event and goes backwards in time. A narrative may also use **flashbacks**: the narrative is basically linear but jumps back to the past at various points to recall important events.

Style refers to the particular way in which the writer has composed the story. Style covers many aspects, such as the use of **personal** or **impersonal language** (see **pages 42–5**).

It also includes, for example:

- how the story is narrated (for example, in the first person)
- how dialogue is used
- if the style is typical of the genre
- if there is a lot of description
- if the composer interrupts the narrative to give his or her comments (called **authorial intrusion**)
- the sentence construction (whether the author uses long complex sentences, short simple sentences or a mixture of both)
- use of punctuation and grammar
- word choice (for example, common everyday words, unusual words)
- whether the language is poetic and imaginative or more matter-of-fact.

If the writer has written many stories, you might comment on how the style is similar to, or different from, the style in their other works.

Sympathy refers to your feeling of compassion for, and understanding towards, a character. You may feel sorry for the character because of something that has happened to them in the story. You may even feel happy for them and share their joy because of the writer's skill. You can feel this way even if you have not had similar experiences to the character. See also **empathy, page 79**.

Tense. You may want to comment on whether the story is told in the present or past tense, and what effect this has. See **page 57**.

Theme is the main concern, issue or focus of the text. The theme is what the writer is trying to tell you about life and living, and will reflect their purpose in writing. The theme is revealed by looking closely at the plot and the characters' roles within the plot. Themes might relate to broad concepts such as love, truth, independence, justice, responsibility or freedom. However, you will usually need to describe the theme in a more detailed way. Some texts have very clear themes, for example, *To Kill a Mockingbird*, a book by Harper Lee that was made into a film (1960), is clearly about misunderstanding and prejudice.

Different kinds of written fiction

Allegories are stories that have another meaning besides the one that is told through the narrative. George Orwell's *Animal Farm* (1945), which appears to be about the lives of some barnyard animals, is in fact about the injustices of authoritarian rule in human societies. The novel was inspired by political and social events that occurred in Russia in the early 20th century.

Contemporary stories are accounts from our own time. The word 'contemporary' is also used to describe a person who lived at the same time as another. For example, Dickens was a contemporary of Thackeray.

Fables are short fiction stories that teach a lesson or moral. Fables usually have animals or inanimate objects as characters. Some fables have supernatural characters and are about supernatural events. The most well-known fables are the tales of Aesop (620–560 BC) which include *The Hare and the Tortoise*.

Folk tales (or **folk stories**) are stories that have been handed down through the generations by ordinary people from a particular culture. Folk tales might include **fables** and **legends**.

Legends are stories about past events that have been handed down through the generations. Legends are not necessarily historical, but people often accept them as if they are. Legends are often about brave or romantic characters in history. The story of King Arthur is a legend.

Myths are ancient stories usually explaining, in a literary form, the early history of a social or cultural group. A myth may also explain some natural event. **Mythical** means existing only in such stories or the imagination, for example *The mythical island of Atlantis* or *The story is set in a mythical town to the north of London.*

Parody. See **parodies** (**page 114**) and **parody** (**page 132**).

Traditional stories are stories that have been handed down from generation to generation. These are usually fiction but might be linked with religious or spiritual beliefs. Traditional stories include fables, myths, legends, folk tales and fairy tales.

CHAPTER 6

Responding to poetry

Poetry generally expresses ideas and feelings about the human experience. These ideas and feelings are expressed indirectly using imagery, sound and other language techniques.

Most poems are written to be read out loud, and that is why sound is so important to their meaning and effect. If you have not heard a poem read out loud, you should read it out yourself (with feeling) before writing your response.

When you are asked to respond to a poem, you will need to identify the kind of poem (e.g. ballad, sonnet) and the sound techniques, language and imagery used to express ideas, and then comment on how these affect your personal response as a listener or reader. To do this, you will need to use many of the terms and concepts explained on the next few pages.

Use the list of terms as a checklist. Ask yourself: *Should I comment on this aspect of the poem?*

Important terms and concepts

Alliteration is where there is repetition of consonant sounds in words near each other, for example *slide silently; crunched and cracked; brittle, broken, bristling*.

Alliteration is a sound technique that links and reinforces ideas across lines.

Assonance is where there is repetition of vowel sounds rather than consonants, for example *twice five miles* (from Samuel Coleridge's *Kubla Khan*). Assonance is very much linked with **rhyme**. Like alliteration, it links and reinforces ideas across lines.

Enjambment is where a thought runs from one line to the next. For example,

Where Alph, the sacred river, ran
Through caverns measureless to man
(from Samuel Coleridge's *Kubla Khan*).

Imagery is a general term that describes ways in which poets create strong visual (or other sense) images in our minds by their use of language. For example, in his poem *To Autumn* (1819), John Keats describes autumn as the season *of mists and mellow fruitfulness*. The description helps us to imagine that time of year. Examples of imagery are **simile**, **metaphor**, **personification** and **symbolism**.

Line length. Lines in a poem may be of similar lengths, or vary from short to long either in a regular pattern or in some unpredictable fashion. The length of the lines contributes to the rhythm and 'feel' of the poem. Modern poems tend to have irregular line lengths.

Metaphor draws attention to the similarities between two things by stating that one thing *is* the other. It is stronger than a **simile**. For example, *The moonlit sky was a blanket, warm and comforting*. It is similar to figurative language.

An **extended metaphor** is where the poem keeps up or repeats the metaphor in different ways throughout the poem.

Metaphor is frequently used in poetry but is also often used in everyday communication. Idioms, for example, are a kind of metaphor. (See **idiomatic language**, **page 51**.)

Metre is a technical term about the pattern of **rhythm** in a poem—the arrangement of words in regular patterns of beat and stress. For example, the line *The splendour falls on castle walls* (from Alfred Lord Tennyson's poem *Blow, Bugle, Blow*) observes a regular sound pattern—the stress falls on every second syllable (this type of stress pattern is known as **iambic metre**). There are various other kinds of metre. A poet usually writes in metrical form for a particular effect.

Onomatopoeia is where the sound of a word resembles the thing it describes, such as *bang, crash, hiss, thud, ring*. The meaning of the word is conveyed by the sound, so onomatopoeic words are highly descriptive.

Refrain is a line or verse of the poem that is repeated again and again. Refrains are common in **ballads**.

Persona refers to the character or voice adopted by the poet for the purposes of the poem, for example, a lover, a father, a friend or a traveller.

Personification is when poets give human characteristics to animals, nature or abstract ideas in order to make the image more powerful. For example, Percy Bysshe Shelley gives the wind human characteristics in *Ode to the West Wind*. John Donne does the same to death in *Death, Be Not Proud*.

Repetition. Poets sometimes repeat words, phrases or lines of poetry for sound effect, or to emphasise some concept or emotion. Alfred Lord Tennyson's poem *1865–66* begins with the lines:

I stood on a tower in the wet,
And New Year and Old Year met,
And winds were roaring and blowing

and ends with the lines:

Old Year roaring and blowing,
And New Year blowing and roaring.

The repetition of the words *roaring* and *blowing* and their reversal indicates the fury of the storm; but it also reinforces the despair the poet feels about nothing being any different despite the 'New Year'. A **refrain** is a kind of repetition.

Rhyme is where the final sound of one word matches the final sound of another, for example *the grave's a fine and private place, | but none, I think, do there embrace* (from Andrew Marvell's *To His Coy Mistress*). Usually (but not always) the rhyming words are the last words in their respective lines. Internal rhymes occur within lines, for example *The fair breeze blew, the white foam flew* (from Samuel Coleridge's *The Rime of the Ancient Mariner*).

Rhyme creates a sense of expectation as we anticipate the next sound and wonder how the poet will make the language fit the ideas in the poem. Great rhyming poetry uses the sounds to reinforce the meaning of the poem.

Rhythm is the pattern of beat and stress in a poem. Many poems have regular patterns of rhythm—a regular beat which makes them sound song-like. Others have irregular patterns of rhythm that make them sound more like everyday speech. See also **metre, page 90**.

Simile is comparing two things by using 'like' or 'as'. For example *As green as the sea*; *Eyes like a gathering storm*; *As much feeling as a computer.*

Sound techniques. Because poetry is generally meant to be spoken or read aloud, poets use sound techniques to express their feelings and to stimulate feelings, memories and responses from their audiences. Examples of sound techniques are **alliteration**, **assonance**, **onomatopoeia**, **repetition**, **rhythm** and **rhyme**.

Stanza is a group of lines within a poem that form a unit of thought or feeling (similar to a paragraph in other texts). A stanza is often called a **verse**.

Symbolism is the use of a word or an image to represent something else—usually something abstract such as an emotion or a condition. A simple example is the colour red, which often stands for anger. Sometimes a whole poem can be one extended symbol. For example, Robert Frost's poem *The Road Not Taken* at one level is about making a choice about which way to travel along a road, whereas at another level (and its intended meaning) it is about making choices throughout life.

Verse can be another word for **stanza**, or it can refer to poetic text in general—for example, *She wrote it in verse* (that is, as a poem). The term is also used to refer to a group of lines that form a meaningful unit of a song.

Different kinds of poetry

Ballads are narrative poems which tell a story, often about a dramatic event or a brave or heroic feat from long ago. Ballads usually have short four-line stanzas and often a chorus or refrain that is repeated regularly. Examples are *The Highwayman* by Alfred Noyes, and *Hiawatha* by Henry Wadsworth Longfellow. Ballads use rhyme and rhythm and often sound like songs. In fact some have been set to music.

Cinquains are structured five-line poems which focus on a concrete image of a person, animal, thing or idea. Line one has one word which states the poem subject; line two has two words which describe it; line three has three words which describe it; line four has four words about the subject; and line five finishes with one word to comment on the subject.

Penguin,
Formally dressed,
Watchful and still,
Egg at his feet,
Heart-warming.

Epics are very long poems describing great deeds or events. Like ballads, they usually tell a story. An example is the Old English epic, *Beowulf*.

Free verse is poetry that does not follow any particular line, rhythm or rhyme pattern. It is more like normal text (for example, as used in a novel). Most modern poetry is in free verse.

Haiku is a kind of Japanese poem about nature. It has three lines: the first contains five syllables, the second has seven syllables and the third has five (like the first).

Still, shimmering heat,
Cicadas, shrill and strident,
Summer in the bush.

Limericks are playful comic poems, usually about a person and a comic event in which he or she was involved. Lines one, two and five rhyme with each other and have three strong beats. Lines three and four rhyme with each other and have only two beats.

There was an old man with a beard,
Who said "It is just as I feared!–
Two owls and a hen,
Four larks and a wren,
Have all built their nests in my beard!"

Edward Lear

Lyrical poems are short poems, usually about personal feelings, which are musical or song-like and have a regular rhythmic pattern. (*Lyrical* comes from a Greek word meaning 'meant to be sung'.)

Narrative poems include a wide range of poems, all of which tell a story. The stories may be serious or humorous, and of any length.

Nonsense verse is poetry about fantastic or absurd events and characters. Nonsense poems usually play with the language and have strong musical qualities. The poems of Lewis Carroll in *Alice in Wonderland* and the poems of Edward Lear are good examples.

Odes are poems expressing the poet's thoughts and feelings about a person or subject, usually addressed to that person or subject. John Keats' *Ode to a Nightingale* is an example.

Sonnets are lyrical poems with fourteen lines, and a set rhythm and rhyme pattern. Shakespeare wrote many famous sonnets.

CHAPTER 7

Responding to drama

Drama is a way of showing human experience through acting and performance. Some drama has a serious social purpose—to make a comment on an aspect of humanity, society or culture. Other drama is less serious and aims mainly to entertain or to amuse.

Most drama is written as a **play script**, showing dialogue and directions for actors and directors. When you are responding to dramatic texts, you may be responding to this play script only, or you may be responding to a **performance**.

Either way, you need to address the broad areas explained in **chapter 5**: theme, plot, characters, structure, setting, language and style. These apply with equal importance to drama.

If you have seen the drama performed, you may need to comment on the visual aspects as well as the written aspects—for example, the acting, the costume, and the set design. Some of these are covered in **chapter 8**, but most important dramatic terms are covered on the next few pages.

Use the list of terms as a checklist. Ask yourself: *Should I comment on this aspect of the drama?*

Important terms and concepts

Acts and scenes. Most plays are divided into **acts** and then into **scenes**. It is important when you are referring to particular events or dialogue that you write which act and scene they occur in. The **opening** and **closing scenes** of the play might be particularly important. The opening scene often says significant things about the setting, mood, characters and plot. The closing scene will often say something essential about the theme. It is often written to have a powerful effect on the audience, as it is the last thing they will see before leaving the theatre.

Dialogue. The dialogue in drama is even more important than in novels, because the narrative takes place mainly through the dialogue. There is generally no narrator to tell you what is happening or has happened—you have to read or listen to the words as they are written or acted. In drama, the **opening dialogue** sets up the situation, the characters and the beginnings of the plot. It orients us to what is going on.

Lighting is usually an essential part of the stage design. It can suggest the atmosphere and indicate when a change is about to occur—for example, a dark set becoming bright might indicate that negative events are about to give way to positive events.

Music and sound effects. Some play scripts include directions about music or sound effects. Sometimes these are necessary to make the action authentic—for example, the sound of a telephone ringing. However, like lighting, music and sound effects might contribute to atmosphere or give a clue to the next scene.

Props are one aspect of the stage design. The props are all the things that are needed for the dramatic action, for example, a broom, a cupboard and lounge chairs. Sometimes the stage design or props might be symbolic. For example in *Waiting for Godot* by Samuel Beckett, the play script gives directions about the stage set: *A country road. A tree. Evening.* The *tree* is interpreted by many people as a symbol for the crucifix on which Jesus Christ died.

Role refers to the part that a performer plays in relation to the other performers and the action. It is different from **character**, which refers more to the personality and background of the person in the play. An actor may perform several roles in a play.

Scene. See **acts and scenes, page 98**.

Stage or set design refers to the way the stage (or **performance space**) has been arranged and constructed for the performance. The written play script will often give directions about the stage design. The stage design generally gives us clues about the **setting** of the drama—the time and place—and the **atmosphere** that the dramatist wants to create. One part of the stage design is the **backdrop**. This refers to what is at the back of the stage—for example, a curtain of some kind or a painted scene. Again, this can give clues to the mood and action of the drama.

Stage directions are the instructions about what the actors should do on stage. These directions are important to consider when commenting on a play script, because they are the only place where the playwright speaks as himself or herself, and not as one of the characters.

Structure. Many plays, but not all, follow a linear narrative structure (see **pages 82–4**). Plays, like novels, may also use flashbacks and other devices to tell the story or to make a dramatic point.

Tension is the force that drives the dramatic action. Tension is generally created by a conflict, a problem, a relationship, a mystery or a difficult task that one or more of the main characters must complete. In Shakespeare's *Julius Caesar* much of the tension is provided by the conspiracy to assassinate Caesar both before and after the assassination takes place.

Different kinds of drama

The list below includes both general terms to describe drama, and some particular **dramatic forms**. Dramatic forms have distinctive structures, dramatic techniques and conventions.

Comedies are dramas that depend considerably on humour for their effect. Many texts (including **tragedies**) have humorous parts or lines, but this does not necessarily make them comedies. The ending of a comedy is normally happy and the main characters usually achieve their goals. In Shakespearean comedy, for example, the play often ends in a promise of marriage.

Look at **chapter 11** to find out how to describe different kinds of humour.

Docudrama is a presentation of factual material (e.g. a historical event) in dramatic form. Docudramas occur in film as well as stage drama.

Dramatisation is the process of transforming a text (e.g. a novel) into an enactment or performance. Dramatisation also refers to when historical or factual events are put into dramatic form for retelling. Again, dramatisation occurs in film as well as stage drama.

Duologue is a play involving two characters only.

Farce is a humorous play involving very unlikely situations—coincidences, and characters confusing males for females (or the other way around) and so on.

Improvisation is a performance which the actors have not rehearsed. The actors may have a basic theme or plot but they do not have a script to work from and mainly respond to the action of other actors (or the audience) to create the play.

Melodrama is a kind of drama that exaggerates romantic or sorrowful events and good and bad characters. You have probably seen 19th century melodramas with moustached villains in black capes, handsome heroes, and beautiful women in distress.

Mime is a dramatic form that uses *only* face and body gestures and movement to express emotion, character, action and plot. Marcel Marceau is a famous mime performer.

Monologue is a speech by one person. In drama, a monologue is a dramatic piece performed by a single actor. The actor may play one character only, or many different characters.

Play-building is the process of creating a play using various improvised activities. It is a collaborative activity which normally involves actors and a playwright, or actors only, although others can also be involved.

Once a play is 'built', the action and dialogue can be written down or committed to memory, rehearsed or further developed for performance.

Street theatre is a theatrical performance in a street or other public outdoor area not usually used for such events. Street theatre often has a social or political message.

Tragedies are stories about serious and sad events leading to a very sad ending—often death or suffering. Many of Shakespeare's plays are tragedies, for example, *Romeo and Juliet*, *King Lear* and *Hamlet*.

Tragicomedies are stories that combine elements of both tragedy and comedy.

CHAPTER 8

Responding to film

Films are made for a range of purposes. Some films aim merely to entertain or amuse. Most Hollywood productions are of this type. Other films aim to comment upon an aspect of the human experience, or to help us make sense of that experience. Many aim to entertain *and* to comment on human experience.

Being able to understand and respond to film is now an essential part of English studies. This is because film plays an important part in our lives. Film reflects the attitudes and beliefs of our time and our society. But it often does much more than this—it makes us think about and even question these attitudes and ways of thinking.

When you are asked to comment on film, you need to cover some of the areas already explained in the section on written fiction (see **pages 74–84**): plot, character, theme, setting, dialogue and narrator are also relevant to film. Some of the terms covered in the previous chapter are also relevant to film because, like drama, film involves performance and is therefore both a visual and an aural text.

The following section explains important terms that are especially relevant when responding to film. You won't always have to consider *all* of these areas, but it is important that you understand them.

Use the list of terms as a checklist. Ask yourself: *Should I comment on this aspect of the film?*

Important terms and concepts

Actors and acting. Who the actors are, and the way the actors perform their parts or roles, is an important aspect of any film. If the acting is not convincing then the film is unlikely to be successful overall. You might comment on how well the actors portray the characters they play. It is important to keep the **characters** and **actors** separate in your mind when you are commenting on a particular film.

Allusions. Some films make references to, or **allude** to, other films or books. See also **intertextuality, page 80**. For example, the animated film *Chicken Run* alludes to the adventure film *Indiana Jones and the Temple of Doom* in one scene.

Cast is the group of actors in the film. **Casting** is the activity of choosing actors for the film. You might comment that the casting does or does not work well.

Cinematography is the art and method of film photography. It is an extremely important part of the story-telling process in film. Cinematographers use a variety of techniques to contrast, emphasise, reinforce ideas and present parts of the story. Some aspects of the cinematography that you might comment on are:

- **Camera angle**—the perspective from which the camera shoots. See also **angle, page 116**.
- **Footage**—a length of film used as part of a film. The term is mostly used when talking about **historical footage** or **archival footage**. For example, the Australian film *Newsfront* used archival footage from newsreels of earlier decades.
- **Freeze-frame**—when the camera stops moving (sometimes used to show a violent death on the screen).
- **Montage**—a number of different shots used together to form a single image. For example, the screen may show an image of a person in one setting superimposed (displayed over) an image of a different setting in the background.
- **Pan**—continuous movement of the camera to record a scene or to keep an actor or object in view.
- **Scene**—a series of related **shots** that usually deal with a particular part of the narrative.

- **Shot**—an uninterrupted passage of film. A shot can be of action (for example, people marching) or a static scene (for example, a garden).
- **Slow motion**—a way of filming scenes so that the action appears slower than usual (for example, showing a ten-second race so that it appears to take one minute).
- **Still**—a non-moving image used within a film.
- **Time-lapse photography**—a method of speeding up a slow process to show it on film. For example, a flower blooming over two days might be shown in twenty seconds.
- **Wide shots**—a shot that allows the audience to see a large expanse at the one time (often used to film nature and outdoor scenes). Wide shots are often contrasted with **close shots** for a particular purpose.

Director and direction. The director is the person with overall responsibility for the creative aspects of making the film. Direction is often thought to be just telling the actors how to play their parts, but it is more than this. It also involves deciding on the emphasis to be given to certain events, and working with other key people (e.g. the cinematographer) to decide how best to tell the story. It is largely the director's interpretation of the events and characters that influences the audience's response to a film.

Flashback is a technique used to show some past event. It often explains the present situation of one or more characters. Some films consist of one long flashback, starting in the present and then going back to the beginning of the story.

Juxtaposition is when the film moves from one scene to another in such a way that the contrast between them is emphasised. For example, scenes of wild outdoor landscapes are sometimes **juxtaposed** against controlled indoor scenes. Juxtaposition is often reinforced by the camera work.

Message. This is the point of the film—what it is saying about life and society. Not all films have a message but many films do. And the message may sometimes be more of a question than a statement. The message is closely connected to the theme of the film.

Music is an important element in film. Sometimes the music may be very much in the background and used just to reinforce action. In other cases the music is a dominant part of the overall message—you are aware of the melody (and the **lyrics**—words—if there are any). This kind of music in a film is called the **theme music**. The written music is called the **musical score**. In the Australian film *The Tracker*, the music and lyrics establish the atmosphere and directly reveal the director's attitude to the topic and the overall message of the film. Of course in some films the music is the main focus—for example, in **musicals** such as *West Side Story*. Quiet classical music is often used nowadays as **juxtaposition** in war and fight scenes.

Pace refers to the speed of the action. Films can be **fast-paced** or **slow-paced** and this can affect the interest level of the audience.

Producer and production. The producer has the overall responsibility for a film's administrative and financial aspects. **Production** is the whole process of getting the film on screen—from raising the necessary money to getting film distributors to show the film in their cinemas. You can also use the word **production** to refer to the film in a general way. For example, *The 1998 production of the film was the best.*

Promotional material includes posters, reviews, advertisements and sometimes objects used to let people know about the film and encourage them to see it. You may be asked to examine the promotional material as part of your response to a film.

Purpose. Films are always made for a purpose. It is important that you think about this purpose as part of considering the message (see **pages 17–19**). Most films aim primarily to entertain. Examples are the *Matrix* series, *The Princess Bride* or *Moulin Rouge*. Others aim to inform us about world events and human experiences. An example is *Rabbit Proof Fence*, which tells the true story of three young Aboriginal girls who were part of the 'stolen generation'. These kinds of films usually aim to make a comment on these events and experiences and may help us to make sense of these occurrences. Most films aim to entertain and comment on human experience in some way.

Screenplay is another word for script but is perhaps used more when the film is an adaptation of a book or a play. For example, *The screenplay sticks faithfully to the action of the novel.*

Script or film script. This is the written version of the film on which the production is based. It is written by the **scriptwriter**. Like the written version of a play, it includes directions about acting, movement, lighting and so on as well as the dialogue. You might comment on the script separately from other aspects of the film. You might be very positive about the acting, but negative about the script.

Sequence in a film is a series of scenes that have meaning as a unit. As an example, an **action sequence** is a series of scenes that build upon each other to climax at the end point—for example, a car chase sequence. A **fantasy sequence** is a series of scenes which shows something that is not actually happening—for example, something imagined by a character.

The **opening** and **closing sequences** might be particularly important. The opening sequence often says important things about the focus of the film and how the story is to be told. For example, in William Shakespeare's *Romeo and Juliet* (directed by Baz Luhrmann), the opening scene is a TV newsreader giving a news update using Shakespearean language from the original play. The next scene is the news camera panning out across the city and then down onto a violent brawl between two street gangs. This opening sequence tells us very clearly that we are going to see a very unusual, very modern interpretation of the play, which will try to make its tragic events relevant to today's audiences.

Sound effects. These are all the sounds except for the music and words—for example, the sound of a train approaching. Sound effects are often used to build atmosphere and tension—for example, the sound of wind and rain in crime or horror films.

Soundtrack. This is a way of referring to all the sounds in the film, including words and music.

Special effects. The use of equipment and methods to create images that are not possible to create in reality. Computers have greatly improved the quality of special effects and they are now used in many films (not only science fiction films such as *Star Wars*).

Different kinds of films

Films can belong to various genres including fantasy, crime/detective, romance, spy, science fiction, horror, adventure and social realism (see **genre, pages 79–80**). Sometimes you will also hear the following terms used to describe films.

Adaptation. When a book or dramatic work is made into a film, it is called a film adaptation. The *Lord of the Rings* films, for example, are film adaptations of JRR Tolkien's novels. When talking about an adaptation, you might have to refer to the original text also—for example, comparing the way it portrays characters, or comparing the emphasis given to certain events.

Animation. This is the process of filming cartoon drawings or other non-moving objects (e.g. clay models) so that they look like they are moving. Some Walt Disney films and the 'claymation' film *Chicken Run* (using clay models) are examples of **animated films.**

Appropriation. A film is an appropriation when it takes or copies another text but changes it in particular ways in order to make a point or to amuse. The film *Clueless*, for example, is an appropriation of Jane Austen's book *Emma*. **Parodies** and **spoofs** (see **page 114**) are appropriations. See also **intertextuality, page 80**.

Classic films are films that have become the standard or model for films of the same type, or simply films that are considered of excellent quality. It usually takes many years for films to be considered classics, though sometimes you hear of a film becoming an instant classic because of its excellence and popularity. For example, the *Lord of the Rings* films are already being called classics. Examples of classic films are *Casablanca* (mystery romance), *Fantasia* (animation) and *The Magnificent Seven* (western).

Film noir. Films in the *film noir* (*noir* = black) genre usually focus on the dark side of human nature. They typically feature dark and shadowy scenes and unhappy plots and characters. The film *The Big Sleep* based on Raymond Chandler's novel is an example. Original film noir films are mostly from the 1940s, but some modern films imitate the style.

Gothic horror is a term used to describe films that emphasise grotesque, horrible, unnatural or bizarre experiences. Often these films are based on Gothic novels. The filming style is dark and gloomy and there are key events that shock and frighten the audience. An example is *Dracula*.

Musicals are films in which music and song (and often dance) are an essential part. Examples are *West Side Story*, *Moulin Rouge* and *Chicago*. If you are responding to a musical film, you would definitely have to comment on the musical score and the singing and dancing performances as well as other aspects such as those mentioned above.

Parodies are films that copy the style or content of other texts or films in a humorous way. Sometimes there might be a serious purpose behind the spoof, but generally the purpose is to make fun of or send up the original. *Shrek*, which parodies fairytales, is a good example of film parody. Other kinds of text can be parodies also (e.g. short stories, advertisements). See also **spoofs** below.

Period films are films clearly set in a particular time in the past, showing the way of life, homes, fashions and interests of the time. They may include historical events, but are not meant to be true historical accounts. Adaptations of Jane Austen's novels could be called period films.

Spoofs are the same as parodies. If there is any difference in the two terms it is that spoofs are perhaps less serious than parodies, and more focused on style than other aspects of the text. The Austin Powers films are spoofs of the James Bond spy films.

CHAPTER 9

Responding to visual texts

Visual texts are texts that include visual or graphic images as a major element. Examples of visual texts are cartoons, text illustrations, advertisements, children's picture books, websites, DVDs, films and ebooks. Visual texts include **digital texts**—texts produced through digital, often interactive, technologies—of which the last four above are examples.

Visual texts usually include words as well as images. When this is so, you should talk about the visuals, but also talk about how the visuals support the text.

For example, in responding to a children's picture book, you should comment on some of the written fiction areas covered in **chapter 5** and then say how the visuals contribute to the narrative, using the terms discussed in this chapter.

You should also remember to look at visuals in a critical way. In other words, think about why certain images have been used—how they are meant to make you think or feel. This is most important in media texts such as advertisements.

Visuals are usually an important part of **multimedia** texts (which combine many media). For example, CD-ROMs may combine visuals, written text, sound and film.

Some important aspects that you might mention when responding to partly or wholly visual texts are explained on the following pages.

Use the list of terms as a checklist. Ask yourself: *Should I comment on this aspect of the text?*

Important terms and concepts

Angle (or **perspective**) refers to the position the composer is in relative to the subject of the visual. Composers choose their perspectives for a reason. Sometimes it might be simply functional—for example, a picture of a town taken from the air for use in map-making (aerial perspective). However, perspective can tell us something about the composer's purpose too. For example, a photograph taken from a side angle might suggest that the photographer wants to show something not usually seen, and to make a point about this.

Background is what is shown behind the subject or subjects. The background is not, however, unimportant. A photographer, advertiser or designer will think very carefully about the background to the main subject or subjects.

Captions are the words that accompany the visuals. For example, a whole-page advertisement might feature a large picture of the product with the company name written in very small letters in one corner. You might comment that this is meant to show that the product needs nothing but the company name to convince the audience it is a quality product. You might also comment if the text contains no words, and indicate what purpose this serves. For example, a cartoon sequence might include a series of frames with captions and then a final frame with no caption. You might comment on how this contributes to the humour (or other effect) of the cartoon.

Colours can contribute to the message of a visual text. For example, dark colours might be used in an advertisement about children in need. This is intended to emphasise their situation and to appeal to the viewer to give money.

Composition describes the way all the elements of the visual are arranged together. You should comment on how effective the total composition is as well as the individual elements.

Exaggeration. Visuals may exaggerate shapes for comic or other effect. Cartoons, for example, often exaggerate the look of characters in order to make the audience laugh or to quickly establish the type of person. For example, a cartoonist might draw male teenagers with skinny, ragged jeans, a T-shirt and a hoodie. This quickly establishes the age of the person for the audience. See also **caricature, pages 130–1**.

Direction of eyes. If there are people or animals in the visual, it may be relevant to comment on whether their eyes appear to be looking 'at the viewer' or at something else in the visual. If the eyes are looking directly at the viewer (as with the dog in the RSPCA advertisement on **page 16**) you might comment that the visual is asking you a question or demanding something from you. The genre of the text will also be relevant—for example, most advertisements attempt to persuade us about something.

Foreground refers to the items at the forefront of the visual—what the composer wants us to focus on. However, sometimes the background can be just as important (see also **background, page 116**).

Frames are the squares or other shapes within which the drawings or graphics are placed. They help to structure the text.

Highlighting includes the use of colour, line, shading, size, symbols and shapes to direct focus to one part of a visual. For example, the cover of a magazine might include a bright orange star in one corner with the words 'Free Gift'. The colour and star shape help attract the reader to the magazine.

Icons are visual symbols that represent information or ideas—for example, the icons on your computer screen that represent saving, cutting or pasting text.

Interactive texts are texts that the user can manipulate or change in some way, for example computer games and some webpages. Most interactive texts are electronic. They almost always use visuals such as icons to make the interaction possible.

Layout or **format** refers to the way the images and words (if any) are placed on the page, screen or other surface. The text may be presented in different ways by the use of text boxes, shading, highlighting (such as bold or underlined words), white space, headings and subheadings, or by the size and placement of the text, words and visuals.

Movement can be conveyed in visual texts by a range of methods. In cartoons, for example, movement might be indicated by lines drawn out from the character's feet. You may be asked to comment on these kinds of techniques.

Perspective. See **angle, page 116**.

Photographs may be used within visual texts such as advertisements. You might comment on why they have been used instead of drawings.

Shapes of items in visuals can suggest a feeling or atmosphere. Rounded shapes, for example, are generally thought to be warmer and friendlier than squares and sharp lines. A children's picture story book is likely to have more round shapes than squares and lines.

Size of the whole visual (or of its different parts) can say something about how important the composer thinks the visual is (or one part is). It can also say something about the composer's purpose.

Space. The composer's use of space is important for achieving their purpose. Advertisers, for example, might use one whole page of a newspaper and fill it with one small picture to advertise a product. The space is what gets our attention first.

Subjects are the people or things that are the focus of the visual. You need to look closely at the subjects. If the subjects are people, you might comment on the expressions on their faces (shown by their eyes and mouths in particular), their postures (the way they are standing or sitting), their clothes, and so on.

Symmetry occurs when a visual is the same on both sides of a central vertical or horizontal line. We call this **symmetrical**. If an image lacks symmetry we say that it is **asymmetrical**.

Typeface (or **font**). The particular style of the lettering of the words in the text. Composers make choices about the typeface they will use based on the audience and purpose and other aspects of context. For example, they might choose a very traditional font (such as **Times Roman**) if they want their text to have authority and look official. They might choose a modern, light font (such as **Comic Sans**) if they want to establish a friendly, open relationship with the reader.

CHAPTER 10

Responding to media texts

Media (or **mass media**) texts are intended to reach very large numbers of people. Examples are newspapers, magazines, radio, television and the internet. Many media texts are also **multimedia**—they combine many methods of communication such as visuals, words, sounds, film or video. Television is an example of a multimedia text.

When responding to media texts, remember that the terms and concepts covered in the earlier chapters will also be relevant to media texts, especially the sections on film and visual texts. For example, if you were talking or writing about a website, you might mention the use of photographs, space, highlighting and so on, as well as language.

A word about being critical

Many of the important terms and concepts that relate to media are explained in **chapter 4**. You should look back at that chapter to recall the meaning of terms such as bias, culture, perspective, society, stereotypes and values. These terms have special importance when looking at media texts. This is because media texts reflect the culture and values of the society in which they are created. For example, magazines reflect the fact that society values fame and celebrity status. It does this by regularly featuring articles about famous people, and by placing their photographs on their covers.

Media texts also have the power to change the culture or society by choosing *what* to write or talk about, and *how* to write and talk about it. For example, by constantly focusing on health and fitness, the media can influence society to change permanently its attitude to regular exercise and good diet.

Media texts are a sub-class of factual texts, but it is important to remember that they are often trying to influence you to think in a particular way about a topic. Even where a text seems to be totally focused on information (for example, a television news report), it is important to examine the text for **bias** and **subjectivity** (review **page 67** if you are unfamiliar with these terms). This is important when looking at newspaper articles, current affairs programs, documentaries or radio talkback programs.

You always need to ask:

- *Why are these people, places and events being presented in this way?*
- *In what other ways could they have been presented?*
- *What is the attitude of the composer to these people, places and events?*
- *What does the composer want me to think or feel about them?*

In other words, you need to think carefully about the opinions expressed in these texts, and how well the speakers or writers support them with facts and logical argument. You also need to question the facts themselves: *What is the source of the information? How do you know it is true?* You also need to think about what facts and arguments have been left out of the text.

Look back now to **chapter 4** if you need to.

In addition, you need to be familiar with the terms on the next pages. Use the list of terms as a checklist. Ask yourself: *Should I comment on this aspect of the text?*

Important terms and concepts

Dramatic language emphasises the exciting (often negative) aspects of events, sometimes making events seem more exciting or more negative than they really are.

Dramatic language is often used in media texts—in magazines and news current affairs programs, for example—to attract the audience and make them want to read, listen or watch more. This is also called **sensationalising** events.

For example, the newspaper might report:

Temperatures soared in the city this afternoon as city workers battled to get home.

In fact, the temperature may have been only one degree more than the day before. And there was probably no reason for city workers to *battle* to get home.

Emotive language is language used to emphasise the emotional side of an event or issue in order to get an emotional response from the audience. Feature articles, newspapers and magazines often use this kind of language to sell more papers. Look at these headlines:

TERROR STALKS SUBURBS

ALARM OVER TAX CUTS

SHOCK DEFEAT AT WIMBLEDON

ANGER ERUPTS OVER RAIL CHAOS

You should look out for the use of emotive language in texts which otherwise appear focused on information and facts. The emotive language will reveal the composer's attitude to the topic. This may make you doubt the 'truth' of the facts. See also **subjective and objective language, pages 38–41**.

Exaggeration and distortion of facts. This is similar to **sensationalising** above. Popular magazines, for example, often exaggerate events and behaviour on their covers in order to attract buyers, with headlines such as these:

YOUNG ACTOR OUT OF CONTROL

CRISIS IN POPULAR TV SERIES

SCANDAL ON FILM SET

Generally the stories that go with these headlines describe much more normal events than the headlines suggest.

Graphics are often used in media texts to make the text look more interesting or attractive to the reader. Computers have made it very easy for writers to include graphics in texts. You might comment on how the graphics support or reinforce the written text.

Headlines and titles are a very important part of many media texts. They are usually catchy and brief, and designed to grab the audience's attention and keep them reading, listening or watching. Newspaper headlines often use dramatic language and in other ways exaggerate events.

Headlines usually make use of very short and colloquial words, for example:

BACKFLIP OVER NEW LAWS

BLITZ ON DRINK DRIVING

JOBS AXED

Paragraphs are short in media texts. Newspapers and magazines employ many 'one sentence, one idea' paragraphs to keep them short and to make the text look easy to read and follow.

Questions directed to the audience are used in media texts to engage the readers and listeners and to encourage them to feel as if the composer is speaking directly to them.

Quoted speech is often used in media texts to reinforce the impression that the news is fresh, accurate and based on fact. Most news reports, for example, will include quotes from experts, witnesses, victims etc. You need to be wary of quotes, however. The person may have been misquoted, which can occur accidentally or deliberately. Often a person's words are edited or taken out of context so that their statement may appear to mean something different from what was intended.

Statistics are often used in media texts. These help to show that the content of the text is factual and objective. You need to think carefully about any statistics used, as they can be used very cleverly to distort or even hide the truth.

Ask yourself:

- *Why are they used?*
- *Do they come from a reliable source?*
- *Are they relevant to the topic?*
- *What do they show?*
- *What do they leave out?*

Structure and organisation of ideas. The information that comes first in media texts is usually the most important, the most interesting, or the most attractive to the reader, listener or viewer. This 'top-down' structure is used because the composer knows that many people only read the headlines, headings or lead-in.

Sub-headings or lead-in sentences are often used in newspaper, magazine and internet texts. These give a clue to the topic and purpose, and set the tone of the text—for example, serious, humorous, light-hearted.

However, they are written to get the reader's attention so you need to look critically at them. Often they exaggerate or distort what the article is actually about. See **exaggeration and distortion of facts, page 126**.

CHAPTER 11

Responding to humour in texts

I have included a short, separate chapter on humour because it occurs in so many kinds of texts, and because it can be quite difficult to comment on and describe. Humour is sometimes used simply to make the audience laugh. However, it is often used for more complicated purposes and it is important that you understand these purposes. For example, it might be used in film or television to make a serious point about human experience or society; or it might be used in a newspaper article to attract the attention of the reader in the hope that they will read on to the more serious parts of the article.

Some important terms to use when talking about humour follow.

Important terms and concepts

Caricature is a visual or verbal description that exaggerates a person's features—to the point where the person looks ridiculous. These exaggerations might be based on physical features (a big nose, a bald head, eyes close together), personality or behaviour (greed, cruelty, stupidity).

Newspaper cartoonists often use caricatures to make fun of politicians and other well-known people. Charles Dickens used caricatures to make fun of many types of people and their professions—funeral directors, accountants, lawyers.

Double entendre (pronounced 'double on-TON-dra') is a word or expression which has two meanings. One meaning is often sexual. A double entendre is a type of **pun**.

Farce is a kind of humour that involves very unlikely situations—coincidences, characters confusing males for females (or the other way around), and so on. The events in the classic TV comedy *Fawlty Towers* are frequently **farcical**.

Irony occurs when a composer says one thing but means something completely different—usually the exact opposite. For example, saying *Nice haircut!* to a good friend when in fact you mean that their haircut is terrible and want to make a joke about it is a form of irony. Irony may also be visual: political cartoons frequently use visual irony. Sometimes real-world events may be seen as ironic, like when a policeman is sent to jail. Irony is similar to **sarcasm**.

Parody is a text that copies the style or content of another text (or kind of text) in a humorous way. A parody is sometimes called a 'send up', especially when we are talking about modern films and television programs (see **parodies** and **spoofs**, **page 114**).

Puns occur when a word or expression which has more than one meaning is used for comic effect. For example, the old joke *What's black and white and red* (= read) *all over?* is based on a pun (the words *red* and *read* sound the same). A pun is also called a **play-on-words**. Newspaper headlines often use puns or plays-on-words. Take for example, the headline END OF THE LINE for an article about young people giving up landline telephones in favour of mobile phones. *End of the line* is an expression meaning 'it is all over', but here it also means the end of 'landline' phones. *End of the line* is a play-on-words using a pun on the word *line*. Shakespeare frequently used puns in his plays. A famous example (from *Romeo and Juliet*) was Mercutio's dying words: *Ask for me tomorrow and you will find me a grave man.*

Sarcasm is a type of irony. However, sarcasm is harsher than other types of irony and is usually used to be critical or even to hurt people. For example, if you went to a musical and were disappointed by the performances, you might sarcastically comment:

There were three big singers in that show and none of them could sing.

Satire refers to a text that makes fun of foolishness, immorality or weakness in individuals or groups in society. A text using satire is **satirical**. The many cartoons and TV programs that make fun of political figures are good examples.

Slapstick is a kind of humour that involves silly actions, for example, falling over, throwing things, slipping on banana skins etc. The old comedies featuring The Three Stooges and Laurel and Hardy were very much slapstick. More recent comedians who use slapstick include Rowan Atkinson (as Mr Bean), Jim Carrey and Sacha Baron Cohen.

Word play is an exchange that uses the meanings of words in a clever way. Shakespeare's plays have a great deal of word play. Punning is one example of word play.

CHAPTER 12

Composing your own texts

This section covers some of the most frequently set writing tasks in Years 7–10. Students these days are asked to write all kinds of texts, for example:

- advertisements
- essays
- short stories
- interviews
- speeches
- play scripts
- diaries and journals
- instructions
- games
- book jacket blurbs
- reports
- brochures
- poems
- chapter stories
- newspaper reports
- feature articles
- cartoons
- webpages
- letters to the editor
- movie reviews
- song lyrics
- blogs

It is impossible to cover all these tasks here, or to give you detailed guidance. You will need the advice of your teacher, and plenty of practice to write these kinds of texts in an effective and creative way.

You can, however, help yourself to write them well by **reading widely** and **taking notice** of all the texts around you every day. Look at the way they are **structured** and the **language** they use. Start a **file of texts** to use as models for your own writing when you need them.

You should also take notice of the way people speak—on radio, on television, on film and in everyday conversation. Pay attention to the words people use and the effect they have on you. Pay attention to the way they introduce their topic and the way they connect their ideas.

Basically the more you are aware of language and texts, the better you will be at composing your own texts.

The next few pages give general hints about the structure and language of some key texts. Firstly we will say a few words about language, and then we will look at some words often used to set writing tasks in English.

Using the right language

When composing your own texts, it would be a good idea to look back at **chapter 3**. Everything that applies when you're looking at other people's texts applies to you when you're composing your own.

The two most important things to think about when doing your own writing or speaking are your purpose and your audience. You need to use language that:

- helps you achieve your purpose
- is appropriate to the audience.

Of course your audience is often your teacher, but she or he will ask you to write texts that have other audiences—perhaps imagined. This is the audience you should think about.

You need to think about all the language issues covered in **chapter 3**, but in particular you should think about the following.

Formal and informal language. Colloquial and slang terms are not usually acceptable in formal writing and speaking. So in preparing a speech or writing an essay, you may need to express your ideas in more formal language than you would usually use. For example, instead of writing *Heaps of kids skateboard to school now* you should write something like *Skateboards are now a popular form of transport for school children*.

You probably know not to use **vulgar** language in formal writing tasks like essays and reports. However, it may be acceptable in dramatic situations (e.g. play-building) or in some creative-writing tasks. But be careful and think about your audience. Remember, your audience might have different ideas about what is vulgar. When in doubt, ask your teacher.

Subjective and objective language. Subjective language is necessary and desirable in creative composition tasks, for example, when writing poetry, stories or song lyrics. It is also acceptable in factual texts where you are expected to indicate your attitude or opinion on a topic. However, it can be risky if you want to convince people that your view is correct. As a general rule, it is safer to keep your language objective when writing most kinds of factual texts.

Personal or impersonal language. Generally, in formal writing, personal language is not appropriate. For example, in reports you need to keep the focus on the information and keep yourself and your reader out of it. Avoid the use of *I* and *you*. In a speech, which is meant to be entertaining as well as informative, it is a good idea to include personal language.

Creative, imaginative language. You will also need to consider it and how to use creative language forms, such as **figures of speech**, **metaphor**, **idiom**, **similes**, **hyperbole**, **personification** and **rhetorical questions**.

These will be especially relevant in literary writing such as stories, poems and song lyrics. This kind of language can help your audience to step into the 'world' you create and hold their interest in that world.

However, creative language forms may also be relevant in more factual writing tasks. For example, they can add an interesting element to a feature article, an advertisement, a speech or a letter to the editor.

Important task words

When you are given an assignment, it is important to understand exactly what you are being asked to do. The task words below are used in many school subjects, examinations and assignments.

Task word	Meaning
account for	explain why
analyse	break something up to show its nature and parts (a topic, a statement, language) and comment on this
annotate	write notes and comments
apply	use information in a particular situation
assess	make a judgement about worth and outcomes
comment	make critical observations
compare	identify and discuss the similarities between two or more things
contrast	identify and discuss the differences between two or more things
create	make something new and unusual for a particular purpose

Task word	Meaning
define	give the meaning of something and describe the main characteristics
demonstrate	show or explain by giving examples
describe	give detail about the features or characteristics of something (place, person, event)
discuss	identify issues and/or give arguments for and against
evaluate	make a judgement about worth and outcomes
examine	investigate in depth and draw conclusions
explain	make plain, say why or how, examine reasons, causes and/or effects
identify	recognise something and name it
illustrate	give concrete examples to show something clearly
interpret	bring out the meaning of something, e.g. an event
imagine	put yourself in someone else's situation
justify	give good reasons for a decision or conclusion
outline	give the main points or features only

Task word	Meaning
predict	suggest what will happen based on what you know
prove	give evidence or an argument to show something is true
recount	tell what happened and when
relate	show the connections between two or more things
review	go over the main points and comment
summarise	state the main ideas briefly
trace	tell what happened, and explain the relationship between events

Sometimes people use these words a little differently, especially 'describe' and 'discuss'. It is a good idea to always check that you are interpreting the task as your teacher expects you to. Ask your teacher to provide you with a glossary of the key words that are used in examinations in your state. The table on **pages 138–40** is based on such lists.

Writing an essay

An essay is a semi-formal, structured piece of writing which makes a statement on a topic or question and supports this statement with facts and ideas. It has an **introduction**, a **body** and a **conclusion**.

Most essays are a formal way of saying:

- *I am saying this to you* (introduction)
- *I am saying this to you for these reasons—X, Y, Z* (body)
- *Now, to remind you of what I have said and to sum up …* (conclusion).

The purpose of many essays is to argue a point of view on an issue, but not all essays are for this purpose. Some essay questions require you to explain a situation or phenomenon. Some require you to discuss ideas on both sides of an issue before reaching a conclusion. Others require you to trace the history of something or to compare and contrast two situations.

On pages 142–3 is an essay 'skeleton' to help you see the basic structure of a typical essay.

Students often worry unnecessarily about the structure of their essays. There is no 'hard-and-fast' rule that dictates the structure of *every* essay—the above is just a guide. However, when you are not very experienced with writing essays, a guide such as this can be very useful.

In most essays the most important requirements are **to present a particular point of view** and **argue in favour of that point of view** by referring to relevant information and examples. The best essays are the

Introduction	Introductory paragraph
	Defining paragraph
Body	Paragraph giving first point
	Paragraph giving second point
	Paragraph giving third point
	Extra paragraphs as needed
Conclusion	

• Write lead-in sentence giving background or context. • Write thesis statement stating main idea or argument of essay. • Write essay map (or preview) telling reader what you are going to write about (this should match content of body paragraphs).
• Define or clarify essay topic or terms if needed.
• Write topic sentence stating main idea. • Write sentence to expand or explain topic sentence (if needed). • Develop idea in topic sentence. The way you develop it will depend on the sentence and the essay topic. You might – give examples – give reasons – give causes or effects – compare or contrast – recount a series of events – list categories. • Write sentence tying paragraph back to essay topic and thesis statement (not always needed).
• As above.
• As above.
• As above.
• Summarise points made in body. • Restate thesis statement or draw conclusion based on ideas discussed. • Round off essay with concluding comment.

most convincing essays: the writer has supported their point of view by using an abundance of relevant and forceful (and sometimes imaginative and original) facts and observations.

Here are the most important things to remember about essays:

- Read the question carefully, making sure that you understand the task you have been asked to complete.
- Formulate your argument by jotting down relevant facts and ideas. Will you be able to provide enough relevant information to convince the reader of your point of view?
- Have one idea that holds your essay together from start to finish.
- Make a statement about this idea at the beginning of your essay.
- Don't write down everything you know on the topic. Instead, choose information, ideas and examples which support your argument.
- Organise the ideas in the essay so that your reader can make sense of it.
- Break up the main ideas into paragraphs.
- Use formal language, not colloquial language or slang.

- Use impersonal language, not personal language.
- Use objective language, not subjective or emotive language (although in a literary analysis, some subjective language is usually needed to express your response).
- Plan, draft and redraft your essay (unless working under exam conditions). It is almost impossible to write an essay in one go, especially without a plan.
- Check your essay carefully to see if your ideas are clear, and if your spelling, punctuation and grammar are correct.

For detailed guidance on essay writing refer to the publication *Excel Essential Skills: Essay Writing Step-by-Step*.

Writing a review

Writing a review of a book, film, play or other literary work is an expression of your own opinion of the text. It is *not* a full recount of what happened in the text. In general, reviews in newspapers and magazines (or on the internet) aim to inform, entertain and persuade. However, you should check with your teacher about the purpose of reviews you are asked to do for class.

Most reviews follow a similar pattern. They:

- begin with a title and/or opening sentence which

identifies the text, the composer, the type of text and genre (e.g. fantasy, science fiction)

- summarise the plot *very briefly*, giving a few main events and perhaps a few interesting plot details
- mention the main characters (and if a film or stage play, the actors who play them)
- comment on aspects of the composer's style; film reviews include comment on direction, cinematography, editing, costumes and so on as well as acting
- conclude with an overall opinion of the text and perhaps a recommendation to others.

You don't have to follow this exact structure but you will generally include all of these elements. You can use colloquial language and even some slang and idiom, especially to make your personal comments. You can use subjective language to express your views, e.g. *engrossing, engaging, stunning*. However, you need to give some support for these views.

The most difficult part about writing reviews is keeping them short when there is so much to cover. It is very important to avoid a long retelling of the whole plot—you will get bogged down and will find it difficult to fit in anything else.

Read film and book reviews in newspapers and magazines and cut out some to keep as models.

Preparing and delivering a speech

Speeches can have quite different purposes. They might aim to persuade the audience to think in a particular way, or to give information, or to entertain.

Whatever your purpose, you need to be informative and interesting and to present your information and ideas in a way that the audience can follow. This takes quite a bit of preparation so you should always give yourself plenty of time to prepare and practise your speech.

Most speeches follow this basic structure:

- An opening that quickly catches the audience's attention and establishes the topic and purpose of the speech. It includes a greeting to the audience, e.g. *Ladies and gentlemen.*
- A series of ideas that develop the topic and purpose—for example, a series of arguments if you are aiming to persuade the audience.
- A conclusion that sums up your main idea. It can be effective to end with a question, a warning or a quotation.

The language you use will depend on your purpose, topic and audience. However, most speeches make use of colloquial, personal and subjective language.

Useful techniques for most speeches are:

- repetition or restatement of ideas to help the audience keep track and to give your speech a structure and rhythm (think of Martin Luther King's '*I have a dream*' speech)
- use of rhetorical questions, which set up a kind of 'conversation' with the audience
- shorter and simpler sentences than you would use in a written text on the same topic
- use of personal experiences—yours and the audience's
- use of first person (*I*, *we*) and second person (*you*) to directly engage the audience
- facts and opinions to persuade the audience
- use of humour to entertain the audience.

How you deliver your speech is also important. So, remember these things:

- summarise your main points or text on small cards
- rehearse your speech a number of times to hear how it sounds aloud and to be sure that you can deliver it with confidence
- look up from your notes as much as you can
- make and keep eye contact with members of the audience

- use facial expressions and body language
- speak loudly and clearly—imagine you are speaking to a person at the back of the room
- pause frequently to give your audience time to catch up
- think of the audience in a positive way (they want you to do well!).

Writing a feature article

Newspaper or magazine feature articles discuss and explore issues and ideas. They are quite different from news reports which generally focus on information—telling us what has happened and when, where, why and how it happened.

Feature articles should be informative and interesting. You may include your own opinion but generally this will need to be supported with facts and logical arguments.

Generally, feature articles have the following structure:

- A headline and sub-heading or lead-in sentence which gives the topic and purpose of the article. This sub-heading or lead-in also sets the tone of the article, for example serious, humorous or light-hearted. It should attract the reader's attention and make them want to read more.
- A series of paragraphs that provide information and ideas. These may be quite short—even one sentence in length.
- An ending that sums up or rounds off the article in some way, for example a comment or question.

The language of feature articles may be formal or informal, depending on your purpose, topic and audience. If your article is light-hearted or humorous you will certainly use informal, personal language. However, even serious articles include some colloquial language to engage the audience on the subject.

Because the aim is to explore ideas, you will use subjective as well as objective language. Again, however, this will depend on your topic and purpose.

Most feature articles display:

- quotations—what other people say on the topic
- evaluation of other people's comments
- rhetorical questions
- humour (in serious articles this humour is likely to consist of irony or satirical comment).

Writing a short story

Short stories are narratives. Their purpose is to tell a story in an entertaining, interesting way.

This short section cannot possibly cover all you need to write a good short story. Have a look at the list of books in the **Other resources** section (**page 184**) to help you further. Also, review **chapter 5** to remind you of the important aspects of narrative writing. Here are some basic hints to get you going.

Narratives generally follow this structure:

- **orientation** to the story (events, characters, setting)

- **complication** (the main events of the story, leading up to the critical event or problem, often called the **climax**)
- **resolution** (story conclusion—the crisis or problem is resolved in some way)
- **comment or reflection** on the events in the story.

Narratives are not easy to write, but being aware of this basic structure helps. Many people find it easy to do the orientation and complication, but then find it hard to write the resolution, and just wander off weakly to the end of the story. Think about the resolution as you write the earlier sections. If you don't have a resolution, your story will just be a recount of events.

Modern short stories do not always follow this traditional structure. For example, they may mix up time frames, going back and forth between past and present (or future). They may play with the four basic structural elements and even leave some out altogether (for example, have no resolution).

Reading widely will let you experience these less traditional kinds of short stories and will serve as models when you want to try writing them yourself.

Generally you use informal, personal language in short stories to make the events and characters lively and interesting. You also use subjective language because a story is a reflection of your own ideas.

Use all your daily experiences and observations as a source of ideas. Many writers keep a notebook to jot down useful ideas—scraps of conversation heard on the bus, descriptions of people seen in the street, and so on.

Write about things you know. This may seem boring, but often a familiar situation or set of characters can at least help to provide you with a starting point for your story. You can then use your imagination to make some changes to the situation, asking yourself *What if…?*

Some important things to pay attention to when writing short stories are:

- Plan your story before you start. You won't usually be able to plan it completely, because you will get ideas as you write, but you need to think about how it will probably develop and conclude.
- Make your opening sentences capture the reader's attention immediately.
- Make dialogue work for you—use it to develop the plot and characters. Don't just write down everything the characters might say in a situation—this will bore your readers.
- Use descriptive language to create images in the reader's mind and an atmosphere for your story, but don't overdo it. Too much description can detract from the plot.

- Think about who your narrator will be.
- Think about which tense you will use.
- Vary your sentence length. You do not have to always use full sentences. You can sometimes use words or phrases only for some effect, e.g. *Strong, sinewy hands. A workman's hands.*
- Avoid clichéd beginnings (such as *Once upon a time*) and endings (such as *Suddenly I woke up*) unless you are writing a parody. In fact, avoid clichéd language throughout your story.
- Draft and revise your story again and again to improve the language, remove unnecessary words and tighten up the plot and character development.

CHAPTER 13

Looking at grammar

Why is grammar important?

Grammar is *not* just a bunch of rules set down by some terrible person hundreds of years ago. Grammar is actually what makes our language work.

If you just string words together in any way your audience will not understand your meaning. It is only because you follow English grammar that people understand you at all.

Knowing something about the grammar of the language can help you express your ideas more clearly, especially when writing. Knowing about grammar also helps you when you learn another language.

It is not possible here to cover every grammatical point you might need. Instead, we will do a quick overview of key grammatical terms. We will then look at some typical mistakes that writers make.

Important grammatical terms

Note: These terms are presented in the order in which they will make most sense to you. They are not in alphabetical order as are other lists in the book.

Nouns are words that name things in our world—for example, people, objects, events, feelings. Examples: *computer, culture, Jane*. Nouns are sometimes classified as:

- **common nouns**—name all people or things of the same kind (*book, grass, essay, girl*)
- **proper nouns**—name particular people, places or things (*Perth, Monday, Joseph*)
- **abstract nouns**—name feelings and ideas (*communication, sadness, humanity*)
- **collective nouns**—name collections of people or things (*herd, team, flock*).

Pronouns are words that take the place of nouns. There are many different kinds of pronouns. Examples: *he, they, it, I, you, her, theirs, those*.

Articles are those important little words *a*, *an* and *the*, used before nouns. *The* is used when talking about a particular person or thing, for example *the girl*; *a/an* is used when talking about one of a general class, for example *a girl*.

Verbs are words describing actions or activities—doing, saying, thinking, being and having. Examples: *run, respond, have, involve.*

Adjectives are words that describe nouns. Examples: *strong, windy, interesting, unfortunate.*

Adverbs are words that describe verbs. They tell how, when, where and why things happen. Examples: *slowly*, *really*, *lastly*, *significantly*.

Prepositions are words that show relationships, for example, of place and time. They go before nouns and pronouns. Examples: *in*, *on*, *during*, *at*, *by*, *for*.

Conjunctions are words that join ideas within sentences. Examples: *and*, *or*, *but*, *although*, *because*, *while*. Conjunctions may join words, phrases or clauses.

Connectives are words that join ideas between sentences and paragraphs. Examples: *firstly*, *in addition*, *furthermore*, *as a result*. They are very important for the cohesion of ideas. (See **page 48**.)

Singular and **plural** refer to the **number** of things being talked or written about. **Singular** is one (e.g. *he*, *boy*). **Plural** is more than one (e.g. *they*, *boys*).

Tense means time, and is used in relation to **verbs**. There are three main tenses—past (*ran*), present (*run*) and future (*will run*). Tenses can be simple (*ran*) or continuous (*was running*).

You might hear the word 'perfect' used to talk about tenses. **Perfect tense** forms show a relationship between two time periods (e.g. past and present). They use forms of *have* before the base verb. Examples include *have run, have been running, had run, will have run.*

Voice is used to talk about verbs. The **active voice** is where the person or thing doing the action is the subject of the sentence (what it is about)—for example,

Henry won the race. (active voice)

The **passive voice** is when the person or thing acted upon is the subject of the sentence—for example,

The race was won by Henry. (passive voice)

Phrases are groups of words that do not contain a verb. Examples: *in the sink, at nightfall, for you.* They add information about the verbs and nouns.

Clauses are the main units of meaning in the language. Clauses are groups of words that contain a verb. Examples (verbs are underlined):
when she <u>grew</u> up; because I <u>want</u> to; he <u>won't do</u> it.

- **Independent or main clauses** make sense by themselves. *He won't do it* is an independent clause. It makes a complete, meaningful sentence.
- **Dependent clauses** do not make sense by themselves. They depend on an independent clause to make sense. *When she grew up* and

Because I want to only make sense in writing if we link them with other clauses. For example:

When she grew up, she left Canada.

I am moving out because I want to.

Sentence. A **sentence** is a group of words that makes sense by itself. It contains a verb and usually a noun as the subject of the verb. Examples:

Don't walk.

If you want to try it, come along next Sunday.

Twenty students sat for the exam.

Sentences are made up of **clauses**. Some sentences are made up of one clause only. Others have two or more clauses.

The **subject** of a sentence is the person or thing that the sentence is about. For example:

Vin studies piano. (*Vin* is the subject.)

State elections were held last Saturday. (*State elections* is the subject.)

Swimming is hard work. (*Swimming* is the subject.)

Common grammatical mistakes

Look carefully through your writing to see if you make these kinds of mistakes.

I have used short sentences as examples because it is easier to see the problems. But keep in mind that it is much easier to make the mistakes, and much harder to see them, in longer sentences.

Look back over the last two pages if you are not sure of some terms used here.

Incomplete sentences

A common mistake is to write an incomplete sentence, often beginning with an *–ing* verb, as if it is a sentence. A grammatical sentence must contain a complete verb and a subject. By themselves, *–ing* verbs are not complete verbs. Look at these examples. (An ✘ indicates there is something wrong with the sentence's structure. A ✔ indicates the structure is correct.)

Having watched the race. ✘

He watched the race. ✔

Having watched the race, he left the oval. ✔

Being interested in music. ✘

She is interested in music. ✔

Being interested in music, she attended the concert. ✔

This mistake often occurs in sentences containing the words *being* or *having* so look out for these especially.

Another common mistake is to write a dependent clause as a sentence, without linking it with an independent clause:

When he arrived. ✘

When he arrived, he said hello. ✔

Because the team played badly. ✘

Because the team played badly, they lost the grand final. ✔

Of course in conversation we often speak in sentence fragments such as *When he arrived* or *Because the team played badly*. Everyone knows what we mean because we are responding to something else said in the conversation. It may also be acceptable to use incomplete sentences in literary works and in informal writing. For example, incomplete sentences are commonly used by television and radio presenters, usually as a means of shortening story introductions:

Fear in the city tonight as gun gang goes on a rampage.

However, in most formal writing you should use grammatical English.

Two or more sentences running together

Another frequent writing error is to run two sentences together as if they were one. Look at this example:

We stopped at the village, we bought some lunch. ✘

We stopped at the village. We bought some lunch. ✔

We stopped at the village and we bought some lunch. ✔

If you are using two independent clauses side by side without the joining words *and*, *but* or *or*, then the clauses must be separated with a full stop, a colon or a semicolon.

This error often occurs when using conjunctions such as *however*, *otherwise*, *for example*, *in addition*, *also* or *meanwhile*.

Changing tenses

In general, you need to keep to the same tense (or tenses) throughout a text. For example, if you begin telling a story in the past tense, don't switch to the present:

He jolted upright when he hears a whisper nearby. ✘

He jolted upright when he heard a whisper nearby. ✔

He crawls to the door and put his ear flat to the lock. ✘

He crawled to the door and put his ear flat to the lock. ✔

No agreement between noun and verb, or between pronouns

You should always revise your writing to check that the subject (a noun or pronoun) agrees with the verb form:

They love their music, and plays frequently. ✘

They love their music and play frequently. ✔

Non-parallel sentences

In any sentence that includes a list of two or more items, the items in the list need to be **parallel**. That is, each item must be of the same form (e.g. nouns, verbs, phrases, full clauses).

To help keep our waterways clean, you should wash your car on the lawn and always putting cigarette butts in the bin. ✘

To help keep our waterways clean, you should wash your car on the lawn and always put cigarette butts in the bin. ✔

Most adolescents say they talk to their mothers about everything from war and politics to friends and when failing exams. ✘

Most adolescents say they talk to their mothers about everything from war and politics to friends and exams. ✔

Using the wrong pronoun

Pronouns sometimes trip people up because they change form depending on where they are used in a sentence.

Him and Jack went fishing. ✘

He and Jack went fishing. ✔

Lachlan and me liked the first act. ✘

Lachlan and I liked the first act. ✔

This problem usually occurs when talking about two people. The easiest way to check is to say the sentence without the other person (*Jack*, *Lachlan*) and see if it still sounds right. For example,

Him went fishing. ✘

Me liked the first act. ✘

CHAPTER 14

Looking at punctuation

Why is punctuation important?

Punctuation helps us to express exactly what we mean and helps our reader understand that meaning.

Punctuation is especially important in long, formal pieces of writing such as essays, where our meanings are complex and where our readers have to keep track of these complex meanings.

We don't always punctuate in the same way.

In a letter or email to a close friend, for example, we can do what we like as long as the meaning is clear. We might use dashes (–) to separate chunks of meaning instead of full stops. We might use double and triple question marks and exclamation marks for emphasis. We might not use capital letters in the right places. When we write a creative piece–a short story, for example–we also have some freedom. But in formal writing (e.g. reports, essays, articles) we are usually not

so free. We need to use conventional punctuation to ensure that our message is clear.

Some useful punctuation strategies are:

- Read your writing out loud. This can help you see where you need to break up your writing with full stops or commas.
- Give your writing to someone else to read out loud. You will know immediately if the punctuation is interfering with their understanding.
- Take notice of how professional writers use punctuation—newspaper journalists, textbook

writers, novelists. Think about why they have used certain forms of punctuation.

- Always spend some time when revising your writing drafts to look closely at your punctuation.

Important forms of punctuation

Full stops

Of course, you know to put full stops at the end of sentences. However, the problem is knowing where sentences start and stop.

A **sentence** is a group of words that expresses a complete thought or idea (see **page 159**). If you look at something you have written and **it does not express a complete thought**, then look at the words before and after the sentence and decide if they can be joined up to make a full sentence. For example:

I gave the book to him. Because he wanted it. I felt sorry for him. ✘

The fragment *Because he wanted it* does not make sense on its own as a complete thought. It only makes sense if you read the words that come before it. So it is better to write:

I gave the book to him because he wanted it. I felt sorry for him. ✔

If you look at something you have written and it **expresses more than one complete idea**, then consider breaking up the words into two or more sentences. For example, if you had written above:

I gave it to him because he wanted it I felt sorry for him. ✘

you would have two separate thoughts. So, you would need to write:

I gave it to him because he wanted it. I felt sorry for him. ✔

Commas

We use commas in three main ways:

- to separate items in a list (e.g. *The three primary colours are blue, yellow and red*)
- to separate a sentence into clauses (e.g. *When Joe first arrived at the school, he felt as if he had landed on another planet*)
- to separate linking words or other phrases from the rest of the clause or sentence (e.g. *Maria, thinking it might help, decided to write Jonathon a letter*).

Quotation marks or inverted commas

We use **quotation marks** or **inverted commas** ("…") or ('…') to indicate that we are writing someone else's words—for example, *Basil asked, "Could I get a straight answer?"*

We may also use quotation marks to show the names of books, films, newspapers and other texts when writing longhand, e.g. *'To Kill a Mockingbird'*. Single inverted commas ('...') are now generally preferred to double inverted commas ("...") for the quotation of words and titles. You can decide which to use, but be consistent within the text.

Note: When typing, you can use *italics* instead of inverted commas to show the names of books or other texts.

Colons

Colons (:) are mainly used at the beginning of lists of items—for example, *I needed three things to survive: a torch, a rope and water.*

Semicolons

Semicolons (;) are used to break up items in a list, especially where some items already have commas in them.

The equipment box contained the following items: a first aid box; one strong, thick rope; steriliser tablets; three small long-life torches; one large long-life torch; and a compass.

We also use semicolons instead of full stops when the ideas in two clauses are very closely connected—for example, *Some people move to the country for the clean air; others move for the lifestyle.*

Brackets or parentheses

People generally use the terms 'brackets' and 'parentheses' interchangeably, so we will do the same here. We mainly use brackets (...) or [...] to include extra bits of information in a sentence. Square brackets [...] are usually used for larger additions such as whole sentences:

Some scientists believe that the Universe will begin to contract until it disappears in one event (sometimes called the Big Crunch).

Astronomers believe that an enormous black hole lies at the centre of our galaxy. [A black hole is a solid sphere formed after the death of a massive star which exerts a very strong gravitational pull.]

Brackets and parentheses are often used to add explanations of technical terms, as here.

Dashes

Dashes (–) are used in many ways but mainly to break up parts of a sentence. Sometimes they are used like brackets to add extra information. Sometimes they are used like colons to introduce a list of items.

The troublesome apostrophe

Most people have to think twice when they use apostrophes. So let's have a go at sorting them out!

Apostrophes are used for only two reasons—to show that a letter is missing (**apostrophe of omission**) and to show possession (**apostrophe of possession**).

Apostrophe to show a letter is missing

We use an apostrophe (') to show that we have left out one or more letters, for example:

didn't (did not)
it's (it is)
I'm (I am)
ne'er (never—in poetry)
he's (he is or he has)
she'd (she had or she would)
o'clock (of the clock)

This use of the apostrophe is not so difficult. One of the most common mistakes is to spell these words as they sound, and forget about the apostrophe and missing letter. So,

dident ✘ *for didn't* ✔

wouldcnt ✘ *for wouldn't* ✔

The other common mistake is with *it's*. See **page 174**.

Apostrophe to show possession

We also use an apostrophe to show that one thing owns or possesses another, for example:

- *the children's desks* (the desks of the children)
- *the sun's rays* (the rays of the sun)
- *the teachers' staffroom* (the staffroom of the teachers)

Knowing when to use this apostrophe and where to put it can be confusing.

When to use it

You ONLY use the apostrophe if there is an ownership relationship between two nouns. Look at these sentences:

- *He pulled the dog's tail.* ✔
- *He put the dogs' food outside the door. (talking about more than one dog)* ✔
- *He took the dog's to school.* ✘

In the first sentence the *dog* owns the tail. An apostrophe is needed to show this (so *dog's tail*). In the second sentence, the *dogs* own the food. An apostrophe is needed to show this (so *dogs' food*).

In the third sentence, the *dogs* do not own anything. No apostrophe is needed. The writer wants to show there is more than one *dog* (plural). She does not need an apostrophe for this. She simply needs to write: *He took the dogs to school.*

Where to put it

There is only one thing you have to remember about where to put the apostrophe of possession. PUT THE APOSTROPHE IMMEDIATELY AFTER THE PERSON OR THING THAT DOES THE OWNING.

An easy way to work this out is to express the words with **of**:

Phrase	**What it means**	**Where apostrophe goes**
the dogs tail	*the tail of the dog*	*the dog's tail*
the cats food (more than one cat)	*the food of the cats*	*the cats' food*
the childrens desks	*the desks of the children*	*the children's desks*
the mens club	*the club of the men*	*the men's club*
the triplets mother	*the mother of the triplets*	*the triplets' mother*
Jenna's project	*the project of Jenna*	*Jenna's project*
Mr Jones house	*the house of Mr Jones*	*Mr Jones' house*

(**Note**: Some people prefer to add an extra 's' to words ending in 's', so *Mr Jones's house*.)

It's and its

These two little words cause a lot of confusion, but just remember these two things:

1 *It's* ALWAYS ALWAYS ALWAYS means *it is* or *it has.*

2 *Its* is a word meaning *belonging to it* (just like *hers* means *belonging to her*).

ONLY use *it's* if you can replace it with *it is or it has* and the sentence still makes sense:

For example:

Mum had the baby last night. It's a boy! ✔

The sentence means:

Mum had the baby last night. It is a boy! ✔

Another example:

The sun is the basis of life on our planet. It's rays give us heat and light. ✘

This would mean:

The sun is the basis of life on our planet. It is rays give us heat and light. ✘

So we need to replace *it's* with *its*:

The sun is the basis of life on our planet. Its rays give us heat and light. (That is, *the rays of it/the sun.*) ✔

CHAPTER 15

Looking at spelling

Why is spelling important?

Spelling mistakes can distract your readers from what you are trying to say. They can also make your readers think that you do not care very much about your writing, or about them as the audience.

Correct spelling is more important in some writing tasks than others. It does not matter too much if you make a spelling mistake in an email to a friend, but it does matter in school assignments, job applications and other serious writing. Note that teachers do not usually expect perfect spelling in exams, so spend no more than a couple of minutes of the exam time to check spelling.

Recognising your mistakes

Seeing your spelling mistakes is the first step to improving. If you are not sure about a word:

- Ask yourself: *Does it look right?*

- Say the word to yourself and ask: *Have I got one or more letters for every sound I can hear?* This is a common kind of mistake, but avoidable. English spelling may be tricky, and often we use more than one letter for a single sound, but we always use at least one. For example, if you write *audence*, you have missed out a letter for the long 'e' sound after the 'd'. (The correct spelling is *audience*.)
- Spend time looking through your draft for possible spelling mistakes. Underline the suspect words.
- Go back and check the underlined words using a good dictionary.
- Computer spell-checks can be very useful but will not pick up incorrectly used words, for example, *your* instead of *you're*, or *buy* instead of *by*.

Spelling words you are not sure of

Try these strategies:

- Write the word quickly. The spelling may come to your mind automatically.
- Write the word a few different ways and see which way looks right. *Basicly?* ✘ *Basicaly?* ✘ *Basically?* ✔
- Write the letters you are sure about and leave a blank for the part you don't know. Try different ways to fill the blank. *D_ vide? Devide?* ✘ *Divide?* ✔

- Think of other words that sound the same and try that spelling pattern. *light/fright/slight*
- Use spellings of related words to help you. For example, the word *finITE* helps you to spell the tricky end bit of *definITEly*.
- Break the word into chunks (syllables). For example, saying *in-dep-end-ence* will help you avoid missing one of the middle syllables.
- Make sure you have at least one letter for each sound. Saying *aud-i-ence* out loud will help avoid missing the long 'e' vowel sound.
- Use any spelling rules you know.
- Use the dictionary only after trying a few of these strategies.

Remembering spellings

Try these strategies:

- Try to remember the way a word looks. Don't only copy a word lots of times or spell it out loud (although these methods can help).
- Use tricks to remember troublesome words. For example, you might remember the IE in *friend* because you have most time for seeing friends on FRIday or the weekEND. You might remember the PAR in *separate* because *separate* can mean breaking into PARts.

- Use the **LOOK–SAY–COVER–WRITE–CHECK** method to actively memorise words:
  - LOOK at the word, SAY it, and really study it—first as a whole and then focusing on the tricky bits.
  - COVER the word and try to see it in your mind.
  - WRITE the word without looking at it again.
  - CHECK the word. If it is wrong, try again from the first step. If it is right, write it one more time anyway, just to be sure. Test your memory of the word every now and then afterwards—in a few hours, the next day, in a few days.
- Put a list of your problem words where you can see it often, for example next to the bathroom mirror. Set yourself targets to learn the words by a certain date. Cross off the words when you know them.

Some basic spelling rules

Rules don't cover everything you need to know to spell well, but these basic rules and patterns will help.

Doubling after short vowel sounds

We double the last consonant of a one-syllable word before adding *–ing, –ed, –er* or *–en,–est*:

- *whip, whipping, whipped*
- *plan, planning, planned*
- *hot, hotter, hottest*

Note: If we did not double the final consonant we would pronounce the words differently, for example *planed* would be pronounced to rhyme with *pained*; *whiped* would be pronounced the same as *wiped*.

We also double the final consonant for words with more than one syllable, for example:

- *permit, permitted*
- *forgot, forgotten*
- *refer, referral*
- *occur, occurrence*

Dropping the 'e'

We usually drop the 'e' before we add *–ing*, *–ed*, *–er*, *–en*, *–y* or *–ous*, for example:

- *hope, hoping, hoped*
- *make, making, maker*
- *noise, noisy*
- *fame, famous*

Note: We keep the 'e' for words ending in *–ce* or *–ge* to keep the 'c' and 'g' soft, for example:

- *notice, noticeable*
- *courage, courageous*

Words ending in short –y vowel

When adding an ending to a word ending in a consonant +y, we change the 'y' to 'i', for example:

- *baby, babies*
- *easy, easily*
- *sleepy, sleepiness*
- *hurry, hurries*

Note: We keep the 'y' if it has a long 'i' sound before adding –*ly* and –*ness*, for example:

- *dry, dryness, dryly*
- *shy, shyness, shyly*

We keep the 'y' if the word ends in a vowel +y, for example:

- enjoy, enjoying, enjoyed
- obey, obeying
- joy, joyful, joyous

Words containing ie and ei

You place the 'i' before the 'e' for an 'ee' sound:

believe, priest, achieve

except after 'c' when it is usually 'ei':

receive, deceive

It is usually also 'ei' where the sound is 'ay', for example:

neighbour, veil, vein, weight

Note: *Height* is spelt the same way as *weight* (learn them together). Also learn these tricky words together: *their, neither, either.*

Common spelling confusions

There are some pairs of words that often confuse people. Be sure to learn these words and check your writing when revising.

- *affect*—influence (a verb). *The film affects many people the same way.*
- *effect*—result (a noun). *One effect of global warming is rising ocean levels.* (We can use *effect* as a verb but it is unusual.)
- *course*—lessons, program. *He is doing a course in electronics.*
- *coarse*—rough, thick. *The paper is too coarse to use.*
- *whether*—if. *Tell me whether I should go or not.*
- *weather*—climate. *It's terrible weather.*
- *their*—belonging to them. *That's their house.*
- *they're*—they are. *They're both swimming in the race.*
- *there*—a place. *She is standing over there.*
- *its*—belonging to it. *The cat chased its tail.*
- *it's*—it is or it has. *It's a terrible day. It's been raining non-stop.*

- *principal*—most important (adjective) or person who is in charge of a school. *She is the principal dancer in the company; The principal spoke to the students.*
- *principle*—rule, standard, basic idea. *You will study the principles behind the criminal justice system.*
- *accept*—take. *He accepts the award.*
- *except*—but. *Everybody was there except Jim.*
- *quite*—rather, or completely. *He is quite tall. I am quite sure.*
- *quiet*—silent. *You must be quiet in the library.*
- *practice*—rehearsal, exercise (noun). *Do your piano practice now.* A way to remember this is that *practice* (a noun) ends with *ice* (a noun).
- *practise*—rehearse, exercise (verb). *Practise the piano now.*

Other common problem words

- *a lot* (always two separate words)
- *advertisement* (think of *advertise*)
- *beautiful*
- *business* (think of a *bus* business)
- *decide, decision*
- *definite* (think of *finite*)
- *excellent* (remember both the 'x' and the 'c')

- *February* (remember the 'r' after the 'b')
- *immediate* (remember the double 'm')
- *interesting* (remember the first 'e')
- *necessary* (one 'c', double 's')
- *occurred* (double 'c', double 'r')
- *rhyme* (remember the 'h')
- *rhythm* (remember every letter—a very tricky word!)
- *separate* (remember the middle 'a')

Of course there are other words that trouble some of us, some of the time. The best thing is to make a list of your own problem words.

Other resources

Pascal Press publishes many books that will give you further guidance about some of the topics and skills covered here. Here are some you could try.

Excel *English Workbook Year 7*, Jane Baker

Excel *English Workbook Year 8*, Jane Baker

Excel *English Workbook Year 9*, Kristine Brown

Excel *English Workbook Year 10*, Kristine Brown

Excel *Essay Writing Step-by-Step Years 7–10*, Kristine Brown

Excel *All You Need to Know About Grammar Years 7–10*, Kathi Wyldeck

Excel *Junior High School Grammar Handbook Years 7–10*, Phil Walker

Excel *Developing Your Comprehension Skills Years 7–10*, Kristine Brown

Excel *Student Grammar and Vocabulary Handbook Years 7–8*, Peter Clutterbuck

Excel *English Years 9–10*, Larry Grumley & Tina Ruello

Excel *Writer's Handbook Years 5–8*, Phil Walker

Excel *Advanced Skills Grammar and Punctuation Workbook Years 7–8*, Jane Baker

Acknowledgements

'Combating that excessive petrol consumption', *The Cumberland Argus*, Sesqui-Centenary Issue, Parramatta, Wednesday 26 October 1938, page 11.

Ladies Handbook, Eulalia S Richards, Signs Publishing Company, Warburton, Victoria, 1943.

'So Much To Tell You' reproduced with kind permission of FurnitureClub 2004, original published in *Blue Mountains Gazette*, 12 November 2003, page 56.

'Waif of the week' reproduced with kind permission of RSPCA New South Wales, original advertisement published in *Blue Mountains Gazette*, 27 August 2003, page 28.

About the author

Kristine Brown is a teacher and the author of the ***Excel*** Essential Skills Series titles *English Workbook Year 9*, *English Workbook Year 10*, *Essay Writing Step-by-Step Years 7–10* and *Developing Your Comprehension Skills Years 7–10*. She has also written many successful books for adult and adolescent students of English as a Second Language.

Index

A

B

C

D

F

G

Q

R

S

T